C-235 CAREER EXAMINATION SERIES

This is your
PASSBOOK for...

Engineering Technician

Test Preparation Study Guide
Questions & Answers

NLC®

NATIONAL LEARNING CORPORATION®

COPYRIGHT NOTICE

This book is SOLELY intended for, is sold ONLY to, and its use is RESTRICTED to individual, bona fide applicants or candidates who qualify by virtue of having seriously filed applications for appropriate license, certificate, professional and/or promotional advancement, higher school matriculation, scholarship, or other legitimate requirements of education and/or governmental authorities.

This book is NOT intended for use, class instruction, tutoring, training, duplication, copying, reprinting, excerption, or adaptation, etc., by:

1) Other publishers
2) Proprietors and/or Instructors of "Coaching" and/or Preparatory Courses
3) Personnel and/or Training Divisions of commercial, industrial, and governmental organizations
4) Schools, colleges, or universities and/or their departments and staffs, including teachers and other personnel
5) Testing Agencies or Bureaus
6) Study groups which seek by the purchase of a single volume to copy and/or duplicate and/or adapt this material for use by the group as a whole without having purchased individual volumes for each of the members of the group
7) Et al.

Such persons would be in violation of appropriate Federal and State statutes.

PROVISION OF LICENSING AGREEMENTS – Recognized educational, commercial, industrial, and governmental institutions and organizations, and others legitimately engaged in educational pursuits, including training, testing, and measurement activities, may address request for a licensing agreement to the copyright owners, who will determine whether, and under what conditions, including fees and charges, the materials in this book may be used them. In other words, a licensing facility exists for the legitimate use of the material in this book on other than an individual basis. However, it is asseverated and affirmed here that the material in this book CANNOT be used without the receipt of the express permission of such a licensing agreement from the Publishers. Inquiries re licensing should be addressed to the company, attention rights and permissions department.

All rights reserved, including the right of reproduction in whole or in part, in any form or by any means, electronic or mechanical, including photocopying, recording, or by any information storage and retrieval system, without permission in writing from the Publisher.

Copyright © 2025 by
National Learning Corporation

212 Michael Drive, Syosset, NY 11791
(516) 921-8888 • www.passbooks.com
E-mail: info@passbooks.com

PASSBOOK® SERIES

THE *PASSBOOK® SERIES* has been created to prepare applicants and candidates for the ultimate academic battlefield – the examination room.

At some time in our lives, each and every one of us may be required to take an examination – for validation, matriculation, admission, qualification, registration, certification, or licensure.

Based on the assumption that every applicant or candidate has met the basic formal educational standards, has taken the required number of courses, and read the necessary texts, the *PASSBOOK® SERIES* furnishes the one special preparation which may assure passing with confidence, instead of failing with insecurity. Examination questions – together with answers – are furnished as the basic vehicle for study so that the mysteries of the examination and its compounding difficulties may be eliminated or diminished by a sure method.

This book is meant to help you pass your examination provided that you qualify and are serious in your objective.

The entire field is reviewed through the huge store of content information which is succinctly presented through a provocative and challenging approach – the question-and-answer method.

A climate of success is established by furnishing the correct answers at the end of each test.

You soon learn to recognize types of questions, forms of questions, and patterns of questioning. You may even begin to anticipate expected outcomes.

You perceive that many questions are repeated or adapted so that you can gain acute insights, which may enable you to score many sure points.

You learn how to confront new questions, or types of questions, and to attack them confidently and work out the correct answers.

You note objectives and emphases, and recognize pitfalls and dangers, so that you may make positive educational adjustments.

Moreover, you are kept fully informed in relation to new concepts, methods, practices, and directions in the field.

You discover that you are actually taking the examination all the time: you are preparing for the examination by "taking" an examination, not by reading extraneous and/or supererogatory textbooks.

In short, this PASSBOOK®, used directedly, should be an important factor in helping you to pass your test.

ENGINEERING TECHNICIAN

DUTIES: Engineering Technicians assist in engineering work performing basic technical tasks, standard laboratory testing or manual work at a field location, with an inspection or field survey party, or with a bridge inspection team, in a drafting room, office or laboratory. You may work with equipment used in surveying activities; reduce and plot notes; trace maps and plans; make mathematical computations and assist with observations, inspections, laboratory tests and report preparation. You may assist in monitoring environmental quality. You may also be expected to use various computer applications in the performance of your duties.

SCOPE OF EXAMINATION: There will be a **written test** which you must pass in order to be considered for appointment. The **written test** is designed to test for knowledge, skills and/or abilities in such areas as:

1. Methods and materials used in the construction and maintenance of roads, bridges, buildings and related structures
2. Drafting and basic surveying, including computations
3. Basic mathematics, including geometric figures
4. Mathematics, including algebra, geometry and trigonometry
5. Understanding and interpreting technical instructions and dimensional drawings

HOW TO TAKE A TEST

I. YOU MUST PASS AN EXAMINATION

A. WHAT EVERY CANDIDATE SHOULD KNOW

Examination applicants often ask us for help in preparing for the written test. What can I study in advance? What kinds of questions will be asked? How will the test be given? How will the papers be graded?

As an applicant for a civil service examination, you may be wondering about some of these things. Our purpose here is to suggest effective methods of advance study and to describe civil service examinations.

Your chances for success on this examination can be increased if you know how to prepare. Those "pre-examination jitters" can be reduced if you know what to expect. You can even experience an adventure in good citizenship if you know why civil service exams are given.

B. WHY ARE CIVIL SERVICE EXAMINATIONS GIVEN?

Civil service examinations are important to you in two ways. As a citizen, you want public jobs filled by employees who know how to do their work. As a job seeker, you want a fair chance to compete for that job on an equal footing with other candidates. The best-known means of accomplishing this two-fold goal is the competitive examination.

Exams are widely publicized throughout the nation. They may be administered for jobs in federal, state, city, municipal, town or village governments or agencies.

Any citizen may apply, with some limitations, such as the age or residence of applicants. Your experience and education may be reviewed to see whether you meet the requirements for the particular examination. When these requirements exist, they are reasonable and applied consistently to all applicants. Thus, a competitive examination may cause you some uneasiness now, but it is your privilege and safeguard.

C. HOW ARE CIVIL SERVICE EXAMS DEVELOPED?

Examinations are carefully written by trained technicians who are specialists in the field known as "psychological measurement," in consultation with recognized authorities in the field of work that the test will cover. These experts recommend the subject matter areas or skills to be tested; only those knowledges or skills important to your success on the job are included. The most reliable books and source materials available are used as references. Together, the experts and technicians judge the difficulty level of the questions.

Test technicians know how to phrase questions so that the problem is clearly stated. Their ethics do not permit "trick" or "catch" questions. Questions may have been tried out on sample groups, or subjected to statistical analysis, to determine their usefulness.

Written tests are often used in combination with performance tests, ratings of training and experience, and oral interviews. All of these measures combine to form the best-known means of finding the right person for the right job.

II. HOW TO PASS THE WRITTEN TEST

A. NATURE OF THE EXAMINATION

To prepare intelligently for civil service examinations, you should know how they differ from school examinations you have taken. In school you were assigned certain definite pages to read or subjects to cover. The examination questions were quite detailed and usually emphasized memory. Civil service exams, on the other hand, try to discover your present ability to perform the duties of a position, plus your potentiality to learn these duties. In other words, a civil service exam attempts to predict how successful you will be. Questions cover such a broad area that they cannot be as minute and detailed as school exam questions.

In the public service similar kinds of work, or positions, are grouped together in one "class." This process is known as *position-classification*. All the positions in a class are paid according to the salary range for that class. One class title covers all of these positions, and they are all tested by the same examination.

B. FOUR BASIC STEPS

1) Study the announcement

How, then, can you know what subjects to study? Our best answer is: "Learn as much as possible about the class of positions for which you've applied." The exam will test the knowledge, skills and abilities needed to do the work.

Your most valuable source of information about the position you want is the official exam announcement. This announcement lists the training and experience qualifications. Check these standards and apply only if you come reasonably close to meeting them.

The brief description of the position in the examination announcement offers some clues to the subjects which will be tested. Think about the job itself. Review the duties in your mind. Can you perform them, or are there some in which you are rusty? Fill in the blank spots in your preparation.

Many jurisdictions preview the written test in the exam announcement by including a section called "Knowledge and Abilities Required," "Scope of the Examination," or some similar heading. Here you will find out specifically what fields will be tested.

2) Review your own background

Once you learn in general what the position is all about, and what you need to know to do the work, ask yourself which subjects you already know fairly well and which need improvement. You may wonder whether to concentrate on improving your strong areas or on building some background in your fields of weakness. When the announcement has specified "some knowledge" or "considerable knowledge," or has used adjectives like "beginning principles of..." or "advanced ... methods," you can get a clue as to the number and difficulty of questions to be asked in any given field. More questions, and hence broader coverage, would be included for those subjects which are more important in the work. Now weigh your strengths and weaknesses against the job requirements and prepare accordingly.

3) Determine the level of the position

Another way to tell how intensively you should prepare is to understand the level of the job for which you are applying. Is it the entering level? In other words, is this the position in which beginners in a field of work are hired? Or is it an intermediate or advanced level? Sometimes this is indicated by such words as "Junior" or "Senior" in the class title. Other jurisdictions use Roman numerals to designate the level – Clerk I, Clerk II, for example. The word "Supervisor" sometimes appears in the title. If the level is not indicated by the title, check the description of duties. Will you be working under very close supervision, or will you have responsibility for independent decisions in this work?

4) Choose appropriate study materials

Now that you know the subjects to be examined and the relative amount of each subject to be covered, you can choose suitable study materials. For beginning level jobs, or even advanced ones, if you have a pronounced weakness in some aspect of your training, read a modern, standard textbook in that field. Be sure it is up to date and has general coverage. Such books are normally available at your library, and the librarian will be glad to help you locate one. For entry-level positions, questions of appropriate difficulty are chosen – neither highly advanced questions, nor those too simple. Such questions require careful thought but not advanced training.

If the position for which you are applying is technical or advanced, you will read more advanced, specialized material. If you are already familiar with the basic principles of your field, elementary textbooks would waste your time. Concentrate on advanced textbooks and technical periodicals. Think through the concepts and review difficult problems in your field.

These are all general sources. You can get more ideas on your own initiative, following these leads. For example, training manuals and publications of the government agency which employs workers in your field can be useful, particularly for technical and professional positions. A letter or visit to the government department involved may result in more specific study suggestions, and certainly will provide you with a more definite idea of the exact nature of the position you are seeking.

III. KINDS OF TESTS

Tests are used for purposes other than measuring knowledge and ability to perform specified duties. For some positions, it is equally important to test ability to make adjustments to new situations or to profit from training. In others, basic mental abilities not dependent on information are essential. Questions which test these things may not appear as pertinent to the duties of the position as those which test for knowledge and information. Yet they are often highly important parts of a fair examination. For very general questions, it is almost impossible to help you direct your study efforts. What we can do is to point out some of the more common of these general abilities needed in public service positions and describe some typical questions.

1) General information

Broad, general information has been found useful for predicting job success in some kinds of work. This is tested in a variety of ways, from vocabulary lists to questions about current events. Basic background in some field of work, such as sociology or economics, may be sampled in a group of questions. Often these are principles which have become familiar to most persons through exposure rather than through formal training. It is difficult to advise you how to study for these questions; being alert to the world around you is our best suggestion.

2) Verbal ability

An example of an ability needed in many positions is verbal or language ability. Verbal ability is, in brief, the ability to use and understand words. Vocabulary and grammar tests are typical measures of this ability. Reading comprehension or paragraph interpretation questions are common in many kinds of civil service tests. You are given a paragraph of written material and asked to find its central meaning.

3) Numerical ability

Number skills can be tested by the familiar arithmetic problem, by checking paired lists of numbers to see which are alike and which are different, or by interpreting charts and graphs. In the latter test, a graph may be printed in the test booklet which you are asked to use as the basis for answering questions.

4) Observation

A popular test for law-enforcement positions is the observation test. A picture is shown to you for several minutes, then taken away. Questions about the picture test your ability to observe both details and larger elements.

5) Following directions

In many positions in the public service, the employee must be able to carry out written instructions dependably and accurately. You may be given a chart with several columns, each column listing a variety of information. The questions require you to carry out directions involving the information given in the chart.

6) Skills and aptitudes

Performance tests effectively measure some manual skills and aptitudes. When the skill is one in which you are trained, such as typing or shorthand, you can practice. These tests are often very much like those given in business school or high school courses. For many of the other skills and aptitudes, however, no short-time preparation can be made. Skills and abilities natural to you or that you have developed throughout your lifetime are being tested.

Many of the general questions just described provide all the data needed to answer the questions and ask you to use your reasoning ability to find the answers. Your best preparation for these tests, as well as for tests of facts and ideas, is to be at your physical and mental best. You, no doubt, have your own methods of getting into an exam-taking mood and keeping "in shape." The next section lists some ideas on this subject.

IV. KINDS OF QUESTIONS

Only rarely is the "essay" question, which you answer in narrative form, used in civil service tests. Civil service tests are usually of the short-answer type. Full instructions for answering these questions will be given to you at the examination. But in case this is your first experience with short-answer questions and separate answer sheets, here is what you need to know:

1) Multiple-choice Questions

Most popular of the short-answer questions is the "multiple choice" or "best answer" question. It can be used, for example, to test for factual knowledge, ability to solve problems or judgment in meeting situations found at work.

A multiple-choice question is normally one of three types—
- It can begin with an incomplete statement followed by several possible endings. You are to find the one ending which *best* completes the statement, although some of the others may not be entirely wrong.
- It can also be a complete statement in the form of a question which is answered by choosing one of the statements listed.

- It can be in the form of a problem – again you select the best answer.

Here is an example of a multiple-choice question with a discussion which should give you some clues as to the method for choosing the right answer:

When an employee has a complaint about his assignment, the action which will *best* help him overcome his difficulty is to
- A. discuss his difficulty with his coworkers
- B. take the problem to the head of the organization
- C. take the problem to the person who gave him the assignment
- D. say nothing to anyone about his complaint

In answering this question, you should study each of the choices to find which is best. Consider choice "A" – Certainly an employee may discuss his complaint with fellow employees, but no change or improvement can result, and the complaint remains unresolved. Choice "B" is a poor choice since the head of the organization probably does not know what assignment you have been given, and taking your problem to him is known as "going over the head" of the supervisor. The supervisor, or person who made the assignment, is the person who can clarify it or correct any injustice. Choice "C" is, therefore, correct. To say nothing, as in choice "D," is unwise. Supervisors have and interest in knowing the problems employees are facing, and the employee is seeking a solution to his problem.

2) True/False Questions

The "true/false" or "right/wrong" form of question is sometimes used. Here a complete statement is given. Your job is to decide whether the statement is right or wrong.

SAMPLE: A roaming cell-phone call to a nearby city costs less than a non-roaming call to a distant city.

This statement is wrong, or false, since roaming calls are more expensive.

This is not a complete list of all possible question forms, although most of the others are variations of these common types. You will always get complete directions for answering questions. Be sure you understand *how* to mark your answers – ask questions until you do.

V. RECORDING YOUR ANSWERS

Computer terminals are used more and more today for many different kinds of exams.

For an examination with very few applicants, you may be told to record your answers in the test booklet itself. Separate answer sheets are much more common. If this separate answer sheet is to be scored by machine – and this is often the case – it is highly important that you mark your answers correctly in order to get credit.

An electronic scoring machine is often used in civil service offices because of the speed with which papers can be scored. Machine-scored answer sheets must be marked with a pencil, which will be given to you. This pencil has a high graphite content which responds to the electronic scoring machine. As a matter of fact, stray dots may register as answers, so do not let your pencil rest on the answer sheet while you are pondering the correct answer. Also, if your pencil lead breaks or is otherwise defective, ask for another.

Since the answer sheet will be dropped in a slot in the scoring machine, be careful not to bend the corners or get the paper crumpled.

The answer sheet normally has five vertical columns of numbers, with 30 numbers to a column. These numbers correspond to the question numbers in your test booklet. After each number, going across the page are four or five pairs of dotted lines. These short dotted lines have small letters or numbers above them. The first two pairs may also have a "T" or "F" above the letters. This indicates that the first two pairs only are to be used if the questions are of the true-false type. If the questions are multiple choice, disregard the "T" and "F" and pay attention only to the small letters or numbers.

Answer your questions in the manner of the sample that follows:

32. The largest city in the United States is
    A. Washington, D.C.
    B. New York City
    C. Chicago
    D. Detroit
    E. San Francisco

1) Choose the answer you think is best. (New York City is the largest, so "B" is correct.)
2) Find the row of dotted lines numbered the same as the question you are answering. (Find row number 32)
3) Find the pair of dotted lines corresponding to the answer. (Find the pair of lines under the mark "B.")
4) Make a solid black mark between the dotted lines.

VI. BEFORE THE TEST

Common sense will help you find procedures to follow to get ready for an examination. Too many of us, however, overlook these sensible measures. Indeed, nervousness and fatigue have been found to be the most serious reasons why applicants fail to do their best on civil service tests. Here is a list of reminders:

- Begin your preparation early – Don't wait until the last minute to go scurrying around for books and materials or to find out what the position is all about.
- Prepare continuously – An hour a night for a week is better than an all-night cram session. This has been definitely established. What is more, a night a week for a month will return better dividends than crowding your study into a shorter period of time.
- Locate the place of the exam – You have been sent a notice telling you when and where to report for the examination. If the location is in a different town or otherwise unfamiliar to you, it would be well to inquire the best route and learn something about the building.
- Relax the night before the test – Allow your mind to rest. Do not study at all that night. Plan some mild recreation or diversion; then go to bed early and get a good night's sleep.
- Get up early enough to make a leisurely trip to the place for the test – This way unforeseen events, traffic snarls, unfamiliar buildings, etc. will not upset you.
- Dress comfortably – A written test is not a fashion show. You will be known by number and not by name, so wear something comfortable.

- Leave excess paraphernalia at home – Shopping bags and odd bundles will get in your way. You need bring only the items mentioned in the official notice you received; usually everything you need is provided. Do not bring reference books to the exam. They will only confuse those last minutes and be taken away from you when in the test room.
- Arrive somewhat ahead of time – If because of transportation schedules you must get there very early, bring a newspaper or magazine to take your mind off yourself while waiting.
- Locate the examination room – When you have found the proper room, you will be directed to the seat or part of the room where you will sit. Sometimes you are given a sheet of instructions to read while you are waiting. Do not fill out any forms until you are told to do so; just read them and be prepared.
- Relax and prepare to listen to the instructions
- If you have any physical problem that may keep you from doing your best, be sure to tell the test administrator. If you are sick or in poor health, you really cannot do your best on the exam. You can come back and take the test some other time.

VII. AT THE TEST

The day of the test is here and you have the test booklet in your hand. The temptation to get going is very strong. Caution! There is more to success than knowing the right answers. You must know how to identify your papers and understand variations in the type of short-answer question used in this particular examination. Follow these suggestions for maximum results from your efforts:

1) Cooperate with the monitor

The test administrator has a duty to create a situation in which you can be as much at ease as possible. He will give instructions, tell you when to begin, check to see that you are marking your answer sheet correctly, and so on. He is not there to guard you, although he will see that your competitors do not take unfair advantage. He wants to help you do your best.

2) Listen to all instructions

Don't jump the gun! Wait until you understand all directions. In most civil service tests you get more time than you need to answer the questions. So don't be in a hurry. Read each word of instructions until you clearly understand the meaning. Study the examples, listen to all announcements and follow directions. Ask questions if you do not understand what to do.

3) Identify your papers

Civil service exams are usually identified by number only. You will be assigned a number; you must not put your name on your test papers. Be sure to copy your number correctly. Since more than one exam may be given, copy your exact examination title.

4) Plan your time

Unless you are told that a test is a "speed" or "rate of work" test, speed itself is usually not important. Time enough to answer all the questions will be provided, but this does not mean that you have all day. An overall time limit has been set. Divide the total time (in minutes) by the number of questions to determine the approximate time you have for each question.

5) Do not linger over difficult questions

If you come across a difficult question, mark it with a paper clip (useful to have along) and come back to it when you have been through the booklet. One caution if you do this – be sure to skip a number on your answer sheet as well. Check often to be sure that you have not lost your place and that you are marking in the row numbered the same as the question you are answering.

6) Read the questions

Be sure you know what the question asks! Many capable people are unsuccessful because they failed to *read* the questions correctly.

7) Answer all questions

Unless you have been instructed that a penalty will be deducted for incorrect answers, it is better to guess than to omit a question.

8) Speed tests

It is often better NOT to guess on speed tests. It has been found that on timed tests people are tempted to spend the last few seconds before time is called in marking answers at random – without even reading them – in the hope of picking up a few extra points. To discourage this practice, the instructions may warn you that your score will be "corrected" for guessing. That is, a penalty will be applied. The incorrect answers will be deducted from the correct ones, or some other penalty formula will be used.

9) Review your answers

If you finish before time is called, go back to the questions you guessed or omitted to give them further thought. Review other answers if you have time.

10) Return your test materials

If you are ready to leave before others have finished or time is called, take ALL your materials to the monitor and leave quietly. Never take any test material with you. The monitor can discover whose papers are not complete, and taking a test booklet may be grounds for disqualification.

VIII. EXAMINATION TECHNIQUES

1) Read the general instructions carefully. These are usually printed on the first page of the exam booklet. As a rule, these instructions refer to the timing of the examination; the fact that you should not start work until the signal and must stop work at a signal, etc. If there are any *special* instructions, such as a choice of questions to be answered, make sure that you note this instruction carefully.

2) When you are ready to start work on the examination, that is as soon as the signal has been given, read the instructions to each question booklet, underline any key words or phrases, such as *least, best, outline, describe* and the like. In this way you will tend to answer as requested rather than discover on reviewing your paper that you *listed without describing*, that you selected the *worst* choice rather than the *best* choice, etc.

3) If the examination is of the objective or multiple-choice type – that is, each question will also give a series of possible answers: A, B, C or D, and you are called upon to select the best answer and write the letter next to that answer on your answer paper – it is advisable to start answering each question in turn. There may be anywhere from 50 to 100 such questions in the three or four hours allotted and you can see how much time would be taken if you read through all the questions before beginning to answer any. Furthermore, if you come across a question or group of questions which you know would be difficult to answer, it would undoubtedly affect your handling of all the other questions.

4) If the examination is of the essay type and contains but a few questions, it is a moot point as to whether you should read all the questions before starting to answer any one. Of course, if you are given a choice – say five out of seven and the like – then it is essential to read all the questions so you can eliminate the two that are most difficult. If, however, you are asked to answer all the questions, there may be danger in trying to answer the easiest one first because you may find that you will spend too much time on it. The best technique is to answer the first question, then proceed to the second, etc.

5) Time your answers. Before the exam begins, write down the time it started, then add the time allowed for the examination and write down the time it must be completed, then divide the time available somewhat as follows:
    - If 3-1/2 hours are allowed, that would be 210 minutes. If you have 80 objective-type questions, that would be an average of 2-1/2 minutes per question. Allow yourself no more than 2 minutes per question, or a total of 160 minutes, which will permit about 50 minutes to review.
    - If for the time allotment of 210 minutes there are 7 essay questions to answer, that would average about 30 minutes a question. Give yourself only 25 minutes per question so that you have about 35 minutes to review.

6) The most important instruction is to *read each question* and make sure you know what is wanted. The second most important instruction is to *time yourself properly* so that you answer every question. The third most important instruction is to *answer every question*. Guess if you have to but include something for each question. Remember that you will receive no credit for a blank and will probably receive some credit if you write something in answer to an essay question. If you guess a letter – say "B" for a multiple-choice question – you may have guessed right. If you leave a blank as an answer to a multiple-choice question, the examiners may respect your feelings but it will not add a point to your score. Some exams may penalize you for wrong answers, so in such cases *only*, you may not want to guess unless you have some basis for your answer.

7) Suggestions
   a. Objective-type questions
      1. Examine the question booklet for proper sequence of pages and questions
      2. Read all instructions carefully
      3. Skip any question which seems too difficult; return to it after all other questions have been answered
      4. Apportion your time properly; do not spend too much time on any single question or group of questions

5. Note and underline key words – *all, most, fewest, least, best, worst, same, opposite*, etc.
6. Pay particular attention to negatives
7. Note unusual option, e.g., unduly long, short, complex, different or similar in content to the body of the question
8. Observe the use of "hedging" words – *probably, may, most likely*, etc.
9. Make sure that your answer is put next to the same number as the question
10. Do not second-guess unless you have good reason to believe the second answer is definitely more correct
11. Cross out original answer if you decide another answer is more accurate; do not erase until you are ready to hand your paper in
12. Answer all questions; guess unless instructed otherwise
13. Leave time for review

b. Essay questions
1. Read each question carefully
2. Determine exactly what is wanted. Underline key words or phrases.
3. Decide on outline or paragraph answer
4. Include many different points and elements unless asked to develop any one or two points or elements
5. Show impartiality by giving pros and cons unless directed to select one side only
6. Make and write down any assumptions you find necessary to answer the questions
7. Watch your English, grammar, punctuation and choice of words
8. Time your answers; don't crowd material

8) Answering the essay question

Most essay questions can be answered by framing the specific response around several key words or ideas. Here are a few such key words or ideas:

M's: manpower, materials, methods, money, management
P's: purpose, program, policy, plan, procedure, practice, problems, pitfalls, personnel, public relations

a. Six basic steps in handling problems:
1. Preliminary plan and background development
2. Collect information, data and facts
3. Analyze and interpret information, data and facts
4. Analyze and develop solutions as well as make recommendations
5. Prepare report and sell recommendations
6. Install recommendations and follow up effectiveness

b. Pitfalls to avoid
1. *Taking things for granted* – A statement of the situation does not necessarily imply that each of the elements is necessarily true; for example, a complaint may be invalid and biased so that all that can be taken for granted is that a complaint has been registered

2. *Considering only one side of a situation* – Wherever possible, indicate several alternatives and then point out the reasons you selected the best one
3. *Failing to indicate follow up* – Whenever your answer indicates action on your part, make certain that you will take proper follow-up action to see how successful your recommendations, procedures or actions turn out to be
4. *Taking too long in answering any single question* – Remember to time your answers properly

IX. AFTER THE TEST

Scoring procedures differ in detail among civil service jurisdictions although the general principles are the same. Whether the papers are hand-scored or graded by machine we have described, they are nearly always graded by number. That is, the person who marks the paper knows only the number – never the name – of the applicant. Not until all the papers have been graded will they be matched with names. If other tests, such as training and experience or oral interview ratings have been given, scores will be combined. Different parts of the examination usually have different weights. For example, the written test might count 60 percent of the final grade, and a rating of training and experience 40 percent. In many jurisdictions, veterans will have a certain number of points added to their grades.

After the final grade has been determined, the names are placed in grade order and an eligible list is established. There are various methods for resolving ties between those who get the same final grade – probably the most common is to place first the name of the person whose application was received first. Job offers are made from the eligible list in the order the names appear on it. You will be notified of your grade and your rank as soon as all these computations have been made. This will be done as rapidly as possible.

People who are found to meet the requirements in the announcement are called "eligibles." Their names are put on a list of eligible candidates. An eligible's chances of getting a job depend on how high he stands on this list and how fast agencies are filling jobs from the list.

When a job is to be filled from a list of eligibles, the agency asks for the names of people on the list of eligibles for that job. When the civil service commission receives this request, it sends to the agency the names of the three people highest on this list. Or, if the job to be filled has specialized requirements, the office sends the agency the names of the top three persons who meet these requirements from the general list.

The appointing officer makes a choice from among the three people whose names were sent to him. If the selected person accepts the appointment, the names of the others are put back on the list to be considered for future openings.

That is the rule in hiring from all kinds of eligible lists, whether they are for typist, carpenter, chemist, or something else. For every vacancy, the appointing officer has his choice of any one of the top three eligibles on the list. This explains why the person whose name is on top of the list sometimes does not get an appointment when some of the persons lower on the list do. If the appointing officer chooses the second or third eligible, the No. 1 eligible does not get a job at once, but stays on the list until he is appointed or the list is terminated.

X. HOW TO PASS THE INTERVIEW TEST

The examination for which you applied requires an oral interview test. You have already taken the written test and you are now being called for the interview test – the final part of the formal examination.

You may think that it is not possible to prepare for an interview test and that there are no procedures to follow during an interview. Our purpose is to point out some things you can do in advance that will help you and some good rules to follow and pitfalls to avoid while you are being interviewed.

What is an interview supposed to test?

The written examination is designed to test the technical knowledge and competence of the candidate; the oral is designed to evaluate intangible qualities, not readily measured otherwise, and to establish a list showing the relative fitness of each candidate – as measured against his competitors – for the position sought. Scoring is not on the basis of "right" and "wrong," but on a sliding scale of values ranging from "not passable" to "outstanding." As a matter of fact, it is possible to achieve a relatively low score without a single "incorrect" answer because of evident weakness in the qualities being measured.

Occasionally, an examination may consist entirely of an oral test – either an individual or a group oral. In such cases, information is sought concerning the technical knowledges and abilities of the candidate, since there has been no written examination for this purpose. More commonly, however, an oral test is used to supplement a written examination.

Who conducts interviews?

The composition of oral boards varies among different jurisdictions. In nearly all, a representative of the personnel department serves as chairman. One of the members of the board may be a representative of the department in which the candidate would work. In some cases, "outside experts" are used, and, frequently, a businessman or some other representative of the general public is asked to serve. Labor and management or other special groups may be represented. The aim is to secure the services of experts in the appropriate field.

However the board is composed, it is a good idea (and not at all improper or unethical) to ascertain in advance of the interview who the members are and what groups they represent. When you are introduced to them, you will have some idea of their backgrounds and interests, and at least you will not stutter and stammer over their names.

What should be done before the interview?

While knowledge about the board members is useful and takes some of the surprise element out of the interview, there is other preparation which is more substantive. It *is* possible to prepare for an oral interview – in several ways:

1) Keep a copy of your application and review it carefully before the interview

This may be the only document before the oral board, and the starting point of the interview. Know what education and experience you have listed there, and the sequence and dates of all of it. Sometimes the board will ask you to review the highlights of your experience for them; you should not have to hem and haw doing it.

2) Study the class specification and the examination announcement

Usually, the oral board has one or both of these to guide them. The qualities, characteristics or knowledges required by the position sought are stated in these documents. They offer valuable clues as to the nature of the oral interview. For example, if the job involves supervisory responsibilities, the announcement will usually indicate that knowledge of modern supervisory methods and the qualifications of the candidate as a supervisor will be tested. If so, you can expect such questions, frequently in the form of a hypothetical situation which you are expected to solve. NEVER go into an oral without knowledge of the duties and responsibilities of the job you seek.

3) Think through each qualification required

Try to visualize the kind of questions you would ask if you were a board member. How well could you answer them? Try especially to appraise your own knowledge and background in each area, *measured against the job sought*, and identify any areas in which you are weak. Be critical and realistic – do not flatter yourself.

4) Do some general reading in areas in which you feel you may be weak

For example, if the job involves supervision and your past experience has NOT, some general reading in supervisory methods and practices, particularly in the field of human relations, might be useful. Do NOT study agency procedures or detailed manuals. The oral board will be testing your understanding and capacity, not your memory.

5) Get a good night's sleep and watch your general health and mental attitude

You will want a clear head at the interview. Take care of a cold or any other minor ailment, and of course, no hangovers.

What should be done on the day of the interview?

Now comes the day of the interview itself. Give yourself plenty of time to get there. Plan to arrive somewhat ahead of the scheduled time, particularly if your appointment is in the fore part of the day. If a previous candidate fails to appear, the board might be ready for you a bit early. By early afternoon an oral board is almost invariably behind schedule if there are many candidates, and you may have to wait. Take along a book or magazine to read, or your application to review, but leave any extraneous material in the waiting room when you go in for your interview. In any event, relax and compose yourself.

The matter of dress is important. The board is forming impressions about you – from your experience, your manners, your attitude, and your appearance. Give your personal appearance careful attention. Dress your best, but not your flashiest. Choose conservative, appropriate clothing, and be sure it is immaculate. This is a business interview, and your appearance should indicate that you regard it as such. Besides, being well groomed and properly dressed will help boost your confidence.

Sooner or later, someone will call your name and escort you into the interview room. *This is it.* From here on you are on your own. It is too late for any more preparation. But remember, you asked for this opportunity to prove your fitness, and you are here because your request was granted.

What happens when you go in?

The usual sequence of events will be as follows: The clerk (who is often the board stenographer) will introduce you to the chairman of the oral board, who will introduce you to the other members of the board. Acknowledge the introductions before you sit down. Do not be surprised if you find a microphone facing you or a stenotypist sitting by. Oral interviews are usually recorded in the event of an appeal or other review.

Usually the chairman of the board will open the interview by reviewing the highlights of your education and work experience from your application – primarily for the benefit of the other members of the board, as well as to get the material into the record. Do not interrupt or comment unless there is an error or significant misinterpretation; if that is the case, do not hesitate. But do not quibble about insignificant matters. Also, he will usually ask you some question about your education, experience or your present job – partly to get you to start talking and to establish the interviewing "rapport." He may start the actual questioning, or turn it over to one of the other members. Frequently, each member undertakes the questioning on a particular area, one in which he is perhaps most competent, so you can expect each member to participate in the examination. Because time is limited, you may also expect some rather abrupt switches in the direction the questioning takes, so do not be upset by it. Normally, a board member will not pursue a single line of questioning unless he discovers a particular strength or weakness.

After each member has participated, the chairman will usually ask whether any member has any further questions, then will ask you if you have anything you wish to add. Unless you are expecting this question, it may floor you. Worse, it may start you off on an extended, extemporaneous speech. The board is not usually seeking more information. The question is principally to offer you a last opportunity to present further qualifications or to indicate that you have nothing to add. So, if you feel that a significant qualification or characteristic has been overlooked, it is proper to point it out in a sentence or so. Do not compliment the board on the thoroughness of their examination – they have been sketchy, and you know it. If you wish, merely say, "No thank you, I have nothing further to add." This is a point where you can "talk yourself out" of a good impression or fail to present an important bit of information. Remember, *you close the interview yourself.*

The chairman will then say, "That is all, Mr. _____, thank you." Do not be startled; the interview is over, and quicker than you think. Thank him, gather your belongings and take your leave. Save your sigh of relief for the other side of the door.

How to put your best foot forward
Throughout this entire process, you may feel that the board individually and collectively is trying to pierce your defenses, seek out your hidden weaknesses and embarrass and confuse you. Actually, this is not true. They are obliged to make an appraisal of your qualifications for the job you are seeking, and they want to see you in your best light. Remember, they must interview all candidates and a non-cooperative candidate may become a failure in spite of their best efforts to bring out his qualifications. Here are 15 suggestions that will help you:

1) **Be natural – Keep your attitude confident, not cocky**
   If you are not confident that you can do the job, do not expect the board to be. Do not apologize for your weaknesses, try to bring out your strong points. The board is interested in a positive, not negative, presentation. Cockiness will antagonize any board member and make him wonder if you are covering up a weakness by a false show of strength.

2) **Get comfortable, but don't lounge or sprawl**
   Sit erectly but not stiffly. A careless posture may lead the board to conclude that you are careless in other things, or at least that you are not impressed by the importance of the occasion. Either conclusion is natural, even if incorrect. Do not fuss with your clothing, a pencil or an ashtray. Your hands may occasionally be useful to emphasize a point; do not let them become a point of distraction.

3) **Do not wisecrack or make small talk**
   This is a serious situation, and your attitude should show that you consider it as such. Further, the time of the board is limited – they do not want to waste it, and neither should you.

4) Do not exaggerate your experience or abilities
In the first place, from information in the application or other interviews and sources, the board may know more about you than you think. Secondly, you probably will not get away with it. An experienced board is rather adept at spotting such a situation, so do not take the chance.

5) If you know a board member, do not make a point of it, yet do not hide it
Certainly you are not fooling him, and probably not the other members of the board. Do not try to take advantage of your acquaintanceship – it will probably do you little good.

6) Do not dominate the interview
Let the board do that. They will give you the clues – do not assume that you have to do all the talking. Realize that the board has a number of questions to ask you, and do not try to take up all the interview time by showing off your extensive knowledge of the answer to the first one.

7) Be attentive
You only have 20 minutes or so, and you should keep your attention at its sharpest throughout. When a member is addressing a problem or question to you, give him your undivided attention. Address your reply principally to him, but do not exclude the other board members.

8) Do not interrupt
A board member may be stating a problem for you to analyze. He will ask you a question when the time comes. Let him state the problem, and wait for the question.

9) Make sure you understand the question
Do not try to answer until you are sure what the question is. If it is not clear, restate it in your own words or ask the board member to clarify it for you. However, do not haggle about minor elements.

10) Reply promptly but not hastily
A common entry on oral board rating sheets is "candidate responded readily," or "candidate hesitated in replies." Respond as promptly and quickly as you can, but do not jump to a hasty, ill-considered answer.

11) Do not be peremptory in your answers
A brief answer is proper – but do not fire your answer back. That is a losing game from your point of view. The board member can probably ask questions much faster than you can answer them.

12) Do not try to create the answer you think the board member wants
He is interested in what kind of mind you have and how it works – not in playing games. Furthermore, he can usually spot this practice and will actually grade you down on it.

13) Do not switch sides in your reply merely to agree with a board member
Frequently, a member will take a contrary position merely to draw you out and to see if you are willing and able to defend your point of view. Do not start a debate, yet do not surrender a good position. If a position is worth taking, it is worth defending.

14) Do not be afraid to admit an error in judgment if you are shown to be wrong

The board knows that you are forced to reply without any opportunity for careful consideration. Your answer may be demonstrably wrong. If so, admit it and get on with the interview.

15) Do not dwell at length on your present job

The opening question may relate to your present assignment. Answer the question but do not go into an extended discussion. You are being examined for a *new* job, not your present one. As a matter of fact, try to phrase ALL your answers in terms of the job for which you are being examined.

Basis of Rating

Probably you will forget most of these "do's" and "don'ts" when you walk into the oral interview room. Even remembering them all will not ensure you a passing grade. Perhaps you did not have the qualifications in the first place. But remembering them will help you to put your best foot forward, without treading on the toes of the board members.

Rumor and popular opinion to the contrary notwithstanding, an oral board wants you to make the best appearance possible. They know you are under pressure – but they also want to see how you respond to it as a guide to what your reaction would be under the pressures of the job you seek. They will be influenced by the degree of poise you display, the personal traits you show and the manner in which you respond.

ABOUT THIS BOOK

This book contains tests divided into Examination Sections. Go through each test, answering every question in the margin. We have also attached a sample answer sheet at the back of the book that can be removed and used. At the end of each test look at the answer key and check your answers. On the ones you got wrong, look at the right answer choice and learn. Do not fill in the answers first. Do not memorize the questions and answers, but understand the answer and principles involved. On your test, the questions will likely be different from the samples. Questions are changed and new ones added. If you understand these past questions you should have success with any changes that arise. Tests may consist of several types of questions. We have additional books on each subject should more study be advisable or necessary for you. Finally, the more you study, the better prepared you will be. This book is intended to be the last thing you study before you walk into the examination room. Prior study of relevant texts is also recommended. NLC publishes some of these in our Fundamental Series. Knowledge and good sense are important factors in passing your exam. Good luck also helps. So now study this Passbook, absorb the material contained within and take that knowledge into the examination. Then do your best to pass that exam.

EXAMINATION SECTION

EXAMINATION SECTION
TEST 1

DIRECTIONS: Each question or incomplete statement is followed by several suggested answers or completions. Select the one that BEST answers the question or completes the statement. *PRINT THE LETTER OF THE CORRECT ANSWER IN THE SPACE AT THE RIGHT.*

1. The basic quantum unit of a two-dimensional computer image is a

    A. bit   B. zel   C. bitmap   D. pixel

2. Noise reduction in a computer image can be accomplished to some degree by

    A. increasing the spatial resolution
    B. using a low-pass filter
    C. image averaging
    D. dissolving the image

3. The specialized memory used for storing bitmaps and displaying them on screen is called the

    A. display list memory   B. operand
    C. video card   D. buffer

4. In computer graphics, the popular *process* color model uses each of the following color channels EXCEPT

    A. black   B. red   C. cyan   D. magenta

5. Which of the following is a specialized computer language for two-dimensional page description?

    A. RenderMan   B. PostScript
    C. Phigs   D. Freehand

6. Which of the following peripheral devices is used as a zel scanning input device?

    A. Shaft encoder   B. NMR scanner
    C. Raster radar   D. CAT scan

7. The purpose of a zel is to

    A. convert an analog image to a digital computerized medium
    B. represent luminance at each point in an image
    C. sample a particular area of an analog image for later digital conversion
    D. store three-dimensional information in two-dimensional bitplanes

8. What is the term for the rotation of an image around its horizontal axis?

    A. Yaw   B. Roll   C. Pitch   D. Slope

9. The PRIMARY disadvantage associated with a *placed* destination document is that the

    A. component files are not actually copied to the destination document
    B. document must be updated if there are changes to any of its component pieces
    C. pointer copied along with component documents is often inaccurate
    D. destination document is not actually complete or integral

10. An inventory of a computer image, which presents the number of pixels at each intensity value in graphic form, is known as a(n)

    A. histogram
    B. frame buffer
    C. matte
    D. look-up table

11. A graphic preprocessor is an extension of the

    A. operand
    B. interpreter
    C. assembly language
    D. compiler

12. The purpose of *instancing* an image is to

    A. produce an analog sequence of animation
    B. displacing two axes of an image against a third axis
    C. repeat the occurrence of a visual object in many positions within an image
    D. represent a three-dimensional image on a monitor or sheet of paper

13. What is the term for the number of pixels used to represent an image from top to bottom and from right to left?

    A. Saturation
    B. Spatial resolution
    C. Intensity resolution
    D. Dynamic range

14. Each of the following is an input peripheral that could be used in 3D point imaging EXCEPT

    A. data glove
    B. sonar
    C. flying spot scanner
    D. laser measuring tool

15. In order to reduce the *jaggies* of a computer image, which of the following would be MOST effective?

    A. Decrease dynamic range
    B. Use a high-pass filter
    C. Adjust luminance
    D. Increase spatial resolution

16. The purpose of occultation in computer graphics is to

    A. determine the edges and surfaces of an image that would be visible from an observer's point of view
    B. provide a dynamic graphic feel that will simulate streak photography
    C. represent opaque surfaces with a range of dark to light values
    D. draws more distant lines with a dot pattern or a darker value

17. A four-dimensional representation of a three-dimensional object across time is known as

    A. planar manipulation
    B. space-time
    C. volumetric representation
    D. animation

18. Which of the following is a 2D pixel input peripheral?

    A. Laser drum scanner
    B. Light pen
    C. Touch screen
    D. Trackball

19. Which of the following is a specialized computer language for forming three-dimensional objects?   19.____

    A. RenderMan   B. PostScript
    C. Phigs   D. Logo

20. Which of the following is the PUREST method for color representation in a display or output?   20.____

    A. Composite color   B. Process color
    C. Component color   D. Multispectral imaging

21. The discrete quantum unit of a three-dimensional computer image is a   21.____

    A. voxel   B. normal   C. volume   D. zel

22. Which of the following techniques produces the visual image of contoured areas of color in what was originally a black-and-white image?   22.____

    A. Tint   B. Dithering
    C. Pseudocolor   D. Conversion

23. A common problem in converting analog images to digital representations is the loss of information resulting from insufficient or poorly integrated image samples. This is known as   23.____

    A. aliasing   B. blanking
    C. quantization   D. noise

24. What type of destination document stores only a pointer at the destination, and does not include the actual component files?   24.____

    A. Embedded   B. Linked
    C. Distributed   D. Placed

25. What is the term for the rotation of an image around its direction of travel through the visual field?   25.____

    A. Yaw   B. Roll   C. Pitch   D. Slope

KEY (CORRECT ANSWERS)

1. D
2. B
3. C
4. B
5. B

6. C
7. D
8. C
9. B
10. A

11. D
12. C
13. B
14. C
15. D

16. A
17. D
18. A
19. A
20. C

21. A
22. C
23. A
24. B
25. B

TEST 2

DIRECTIONS: Each question or incomplete statement is followed by several suggested answers or completions. Select the one that BEST answers the question or completes the statement. *PRINT THE LETTER OF THE CORRECT ANSWER IN THE SPACE AT THE RIGHT.*

1. Which type of specialized rendering of an object allows the observer to view an image "dead on"? _____ projection. 1._____

    A. orthogonal
    B. axonometric
    C. oblique
    D. perspective

2. Which of the following is a means for defining two-dimensional locations in terms of an angle and a radius? 2._____

    A. Orthogonal distances
    B. Polar coordinates
    C. Cartesian coordinates
    D. Altazimuthal coordinates

3. The output for voxel input devices would MOST likely take the form of 3._____

    A. stereo lithography
    B. a printer
    C. a vibrating display
    D. a video raster CRT

4. The orientation of a three-dimensional computer image's surface is described by the direction it is facing, or its 4._____

    A. vector
    B. pitch
    C. stellation
    D. normal

5. The HLS color model is useful in computer graphics because 5._____

    A. the gray level will automatically change in proportion to adjustments in saturation
    B. it allows transparent composite images to show through
    C. it permits luminance to be manipulated as a variable independent of hue and saturation
    D. it permits the application of multispectral imaging

6. The number of frames or points that can be displayed per second by a peripheral system is expressed in terms of 6._____

    A. luminance
    B. spatial resolution
    C. saturation
    D. temporal resolution

7. What is the term for a pixel array that is smaller than the total area of a picture, and which functions as a submodule? 7._____

    A. Cell
    B. Strobe
    C. Sprite
    D. Matte

8. A _____ is a pixel input peripheral that will record images as pixels directly onto a floppy disk. 8._____

    A. flat bed scanner
    B. video still camera
    C. photogram
    D. video scanner

9. The number of horizontal pixels in an image, divided by the number of vertical pixels, will produce the image's

   A. aspect ratio
   B. slope
   C. raster
   D. resolution

10. Which of the following techniques is used to maintain the total color information of an image while representing it with fewer colors?

    A. Tint
    B. Dithering
    C. Pseudocolor
    D. Conversion

11. The MOST common spatial-aliasing effect encountered in computer-generated images is

    A. noise
    B. blanking
    C. jaggies
    D. moire pattern

12. The number of dots in a computer image is expressed in terms of

    A. luminance
    B. spatial resolution
    C. saturation
    D. temporal resolution

13. The MAIN difference between drop shadows and extrusions is that

    A. extrusions extend into space and are three-dimensional
    B. drop shadows are concerned only with vertical axes
    C. extrusions are instanced to a greater extent
    D. drop shadows are used for 3D imaging only

14. The entire matrix of pixels in an image is known as the

    A. bitplane
    B. array
    C. bitmap
    D. tessellation

15. What is the term for a bitmap that records the transparency of an image at each pixel?

    A. Alpha channel
    B. Matte
    C. Operand
    D. Composite

16. Which of the following is a specialized computer program for manipulating two-dimensional images?

    A. Freehand
    B. QuickDraw
    C. Photoshop
    D. Phigs

17. Which of the following is NOT classified as a *subtractive* primary color?

    A. Yellow   B. Orange   C. Magenta   D. Cyan

18. What type of destination document stores both the component files and a pointer to each of the source applications?

    A. Embedded
    B. Linked
    C. Distributed
    D. Placed

19. Which of the following techniques enlarges or reduces the number of pixels that define an image? 19.____

    A. Scan conversion B. Scaling
    C. Scrolling D. Spatial resolution

20. Which of the following is a means for defining three-dimensional locations in terms of two angles and one magnitude? 20.____

    A. Orthogonal distances
    B. Polar coordinates
    C. Cartesian coordinates
    D. Altazimuthal coordinates

21. Each of the following is an output peripheral that can be used in 2D pixel imaging EXCEPT a 21.____

    A. dot matrix printer B. multiplex hologram
    C. thermal wax plotter D. film recorder

22. Which of the following is a function of how many bits are stored in each pixel of an image? 22.____

    A. Spatial resolution B. Contrast
    C. Dynamic range D. Saturation

23. What is the term for the rotation of an image around its vertical axis? 23.____

    A. Yaw B. Roll C. Pitch D. Slope

24. A(n) _____ projection is a type of specialized rendering of an object which scales distances along three axes. 24.____

    A. orthogonal B. isometric
    C. oblique D. perspective

25. The number of gray levels or colors in an image is expressed in terms of 25.____

    A. luminance B. spatial resolution
    C. saturation D. temporal resolution

KEY (CORRECT ANSWERS)

1. A
2. B
3. A
4. D
5. C

6. D
7. C
8. B
9. A
10. B

11. C
12. B
13. A
14. C
15. B

16. C
17. B
18. A
19. B
20. B

21. B
22. C
23. A
24. B
25. A

———

EXAMINATION SECTION
TEST 1

DIRECTIONS: Each question or incomplete statement is followed by several suggested answers or completions. Select the one that BEST answers the question or completes the statement. *PRINT THE LETTER OF THE CORRECT ANSWER IN THE SPACE AT THE RIGHT.*

1. Computer graphic programming is concerned with
   A. animation
   B. pixel addressing
   C. color representation
   D. all of the above

   1.____

2. DIB is an abbreviation for
   A. data input button
   B. data dependent bitmap
   C. device independent bitmap
   D. none of the above

   2.____

3. Computer graphics can be categorized into
   A. real time
   B. interactive
   C. photo-realistic
   D. all of the above

   3.____

4. DIB are used as native graphics for
   A. Windows Embedded CE
   B. Directx
   C. both A and B
   D. none of the above

   4.____

5. An image is _____ of pixel which varies in colors.
   A. triangle
   B. rectangle
   C. circle
   D. all of the above

   5.____

6. Graphic software deals with
   A. images
   B. animations
   C. architecture
   D. all of the above

   6.____

7. Skencil is a program which is developed for
   A. Unix
   B. Linux
   C. none of the above
   D. both A and B

   7.____

8. 3D Plus is suitable for _____ jobs.
   A. small
   B. quick
   C. long
   D. all of the above

   8.____

9. An important characteristic of digital cameras is
   A. speed
   B. portability
   C. non-contact digitizing
   D. all of the above

   9.____

10. Snap is a function of AutoCAD which is used to _____ fixed points.
    A. add
    B. delete
    C. maintain
    D. all of the above

11. Engineering drawings include
    A. isometric
    B. orthographic
    C. dimensioning
    D. all of the above

12. Drafting is another name of _____ drawing.
    A. technical
    B. engineering
    C. complex
    D. all of the above

13. Architectural models represent _____ design.
    A. technical
    B. engineering
    C. architectural
    D. none of the above

14. Base maps represent physical features like
    A. street grids
    B. river locations
    C. landscapes
    D. all of the above

15. Two major types of base maps are
    A. skeleton base maps
    B. country and township base maps
    C. interior maps
    D. A and B only

16. Abstraction is the most important phase in the _____ process.
    A. development
    B. design
    C. both A and B
    D. none of the above

17. In the design process, _____ helps in redesigning.
    A. abstraction
    B. models
    C. simulation
    D. all of the above

18. Prerequisites for logical design are
    A. business analysis
    B. technical requirements
    C. both A and B
    D. none of the above

19. A graphics technician maintains records in the form of
    A. print orders
    B. billing files
    C. maintenance agreements
    D. all of the above

20. Technical drawing requires intensive
    A. communication
    B. expertise
    C. both A and B
    D. none of the above

21. A computer graphic technician is responsible for
    A. concepts
    B. interpretation of design
    C. both A and B
    D. none of the above

22. A computer graphic technician deals with
    A. advertising   B. marketing
    C. multimedia publishing   D. all of the above

23. A graphic technician should have communication with a
    A. graphic designer   B. requirement engineer
    C. project manager   D. all of the above

24. Interdisciplinary environment is important for a
    A. graphic technician   B. graphic designer
    C. none of the above   D. both A and B

25. A graphic technician must be
    A. a team player   B. challenging
    C. innovative   D. all of the above

KEY (CORRECT ANSWERS)

1.	D	11.	D
2.	C	12.	A
3.	D	13.	C
4.	C	14.	D
5.	B	15.	D
6.	D	16.	B
7.	D	17.	C
8.	A	18.	C
9.	D	19.	D
10.	A	20.	A

21. C
22. D
23. D
24. A
25. D

TEST 2

DIRECTIONS: Each question or incomplete statement is followed by several suggested answers or completions. Select the one that BEST answers the question or completes the statement. *PRINT THE LETTER OF THE CORRECT ANSWER IN THE SPACE AT THE RIGHT.*

1. Visual unity is a basic goal for _____ design. 1._____
   A. graphic
   B. web
   C. architecture
   D. both A and B

2. _____ is an important element of good graphic design. 2._____
   A. color
   B. hierarchy
   C. image
   D. all of the above

3. Graphics designing is based on _____ of design. 3._____
   A. elements
   B. principles
   C. none of the above
   D. both A and B

4. Normally there are _____ elements of design. 4._____
   A. 5
   B. 2
   C. 6
   D. none of the above

5. Proximity is part of _____ of design. 5._____
   A. principles
   B. elements
   C. none of the above
   D. both A and B

6. Computer graphics can be divided into _____ groups. 6._____
   A. 2   B. 6   C. 5   D. 3

7. The basic shapes used in graphic design are 7._____
   A. circle
   B. square
   C. triangle
   D. all of the above

8. Positive and negative space must be considered in every 8._____
   A. concept
   B. design
   C. element
   D. none of the above

9. _____ is the critical aspect of graphic design. 9._____
   A. Size
   B. Shape
   C. Color
   D. None of the above

10. Graphical representations are _____ of textual content. 10._____
    A. images
    B. illustrations
    C. both A and B
    D. all of the above

11. An architectural model is a(n) _____ model.
    A. engineering
    B. complex
    C. scale
    D. all of the above

12. Presentation, fundraising, and obtaining permits can be shown by a(n) _____ model.
    A. software
    B. engineering
    C. architectural
    D. all of the above

13. Urban models are one of the _____ models.
    A. engineering
    B. scientific
    C. architectural
    D. none of the above

14. In industry and engineering, ideas are represented by
    A. design
    B. images
    C. technical drawings
    D. none of the above

15. Computer aided designs are of _____ types.
    A. five
    B. two
    C. three
    D. none of the above

16. _____ graphics are the easy way to present complex technical information.
    A. technical
    B. simple
    C. complex
    D. all of the above

17. _____ is an architecture design software.
    A. Photoshop
    B. Sketch Up
    C. None of the above
    D. Both A and B

18. Translating complex drawings into creative models is a(n) _____ task.
    A. challenging
    B. innovative
    C. important
    D. all of the above

19. Drawing tools assist in
    A. layout
    B. speed
    C. both A and B
    D. none of the above

20. Technical drawings can BEST be drawn by
    A. Autodesk
    B. Softimage
    C. both A and B
    D. none of the above

21. A graphic technician must have _____ skills.
    A. technical
    B. design
    C. both A and B
    D. none of the above

22. Information communication can help in resolving complex _____ issues.
    A. design
    B. technical
    C. architectural
    D. all of the above

23. A graphic technician collaborates with
    A. a team
    B. stakeholders
    C. technical persons
    D. all of the above

23.____

24. _____ are also prepared by a graphic technician.
    A. Presentations
    B. Bitmap
    C. None of the above
    D. Both A and B

24.____

25. A graphic technician works under the supervision of
    A. an engineer
    B. architect
    C. graphic supervisor
    D. all of the above

25.____

KEY (CORRECT ANSWERS)

1.	A		11.	C
2.	B		12.	C
3.	D		13.	C
4.	C		14.	C
5.	A		15.	B
6.	A		16.	B
7.	D		17.	B
8.	B		18.	D
9.	C		19.	C
10.	A		20.	A

21. C
22. D
23. D
24. A
25. C

TEST 3

DIRECTIONS: Each question or incomplete statement is followed by several suggested answers or completions. Select the one that BEST answers the question or completes the statement. *PRINT THE LETTER OF THE CORRECT ANSWER IN THE SPACE AT THE RIGHT.*

1. Graphic representations include
   A. concept maps
   B. comparison
   C. process
   D. all of the above

   1.____

2. Similarity is an important concern of design
   A. principle
   B. web designer
   C. computer graphic technician
   D. A and B only

   2.____

3. 3D computer graphics depend on _____ images.
   A. raster
   B. vector
   C. bitmap
   D. both A and B

   3.____

4. A three-dimensional object can be represented by a(n) _____ model.
   A. 3D
   B. technical
   C. engineering
   D. all of the above

   4.____

5. _____ is the best way to convert a model into an image.
   A. Drafting
   B. Rendering
   C. Drawing
   D. All of the above

   5.____

6. 3D modeling software includes
   A. Blender
   B. Art of Illusion
   C. Softimage
   D. all of the above

   6.____

7. AutoCAD is concerned with
   A. drafting
   B. developing
   C. customizing
   D. all of the above

   7.____

8. To open a 2D drawing in a 3D program, _____ file extension works well.
   A. DWG
   B. GIF
   C. PNG
   D. all of the above

   8.____

9. Paper design is replaced by
   A. AutoCAD
   B. Microstation
   C. none of the above
   D. both A and B

   9.____

10. _____ demonstrates 2D and 3D modeling.
    A. Drafting
    B. Designing
    C. None of the above
    D. All of the above

    10.____

11. Architects use architectural models because models provide
    A. quick understanding
    B. efficiency
    C. easy demonstration
    D. all of the above

    11.____

12. Which of the following types of model is normally used for landscape modeling?
    A. Interior model
    B. Exterior model
    C. Urban model
    D. All of the above

    12.____

13. Prototyping technologies are normally _____ based.
    A. modeling
    B. Photoshop
    C. CAD
    D. all of the above

    13.____

14. In an isometric model, object lines are always drawn
    A. vertically
    B. horizontally
    C. parallel
    D. all of the above

    14.____

15. Hidden components of a device are shown by _____ through technical drawing.
    A. AutoCAD
    B. Cross-sectional view
    C. Both A and B
    D. none of the above

    15.____

16. A technical drawing has _____ basic applications.
    A. two
    B. five
    C. three
    D. none of the above

    16.____

17. Full section view in architectural design is known as
    A. dimension
    B. plan
    C. axis
    D. all of the above

    17.____

18. Engineering drawings are concerned with
    A. layout
    B. interpretation
    C. appearance
    A. all of the above

    18.____

19. Two types of technical drawings which are based on graphic projection are
    A. two-dimensional representation
    B. three-dimensional representation
    C. both A and B
    D. none of the above

    19.____

20. Interior models are concerned with
    A. space planning
    B. furniture
    C. colors
    D. all of the above

    20.____

21. A graphic technician should be aware of
    A. principles
    B. processes
    C. equipment
    D. all of the above

    21.____

22. Interpersonal skills are important to learn for   22.____
    A. graphics technician   B. web designer
    C. project manager   D. all of the above

23. Record keeping techniques are defined by   23.____
    A. stakeholders   B. graphic designers
    C. graphic technicians   D. all of the above

24. Maintenance of equipment is important to keep   24.____
    A. data   B. records
    C. none of the above   D. both A and B

25. _____ communication is an important concern of the design phase.   25.____
    A. Oral   B. Written
    C. Both A and B   D. None of the above

KEY (CORRECT ANSWERS)

1.	D	11.	D
2.	A	12.	B
3.	D	13.	C
4.	A	14.	A
5.	B	15.	B
6.	D	16.	A
7.	D	17.	B
8.	A	18.	D
9.	D	19.	C
10.	A	20.	D

21. D
22. D
23. C
24. B
25. D

TEST 4

DIRECTIONS: Each question or incomplete statement is followed by several suggested answers or completions. Select the one that BEST answers the question or completes the statement. *PRINT THE LETTER OF THE CORRECT ANSWER IN THE SPACE AT THE RIGHT.*

1. Design elements include
   A. attributes   B. shapes
   C. architecture   D. all of the above   1._____

2. Tactile texture provides _____ dimensional impression of the surface.
   A. two   B. three
   C. one   D. all of the above   2._____

3. Space is an important concern of design which includes
   A. overlap   B. shading
   C. highlight   D. all of the above   3._____

4. Repetition and continuation are methods of _____ design.
   A. elements   B. both A and C
   C. principles   D. all of the above   4._____

5. Direction and texture are _____ of design.
   A. elements   B. rules
   C. both A and B   D. all of the above   5._____

6. Architecture design is handled through
   A. CAD   B. CAAD
   C. AutoCAD   D. all of the above   6._____

7. _____ is used for 3D architecture of homes.
   A. Photoshop   B. Autodesk
   C. Chief architect   D. All of the above   7._____

8. Autodesk has the ability to provide
   A. innovation   B. visualization
   C. simulation   D. all of the above   8._____

9. Building information modeling is the modern drift in
   A. architecture   B. engineering
   C. construction   D. all of the above   9._____

10. _____ is a software tool for business information modeling.
   A. Archicad   B. AutoCAD
   C. Illustrator   D. All of the above   10._____

11. Home, kitchen, baths, and interiors are BEST designed by   11._____
    A. home designer suit   B. Archicad
    C. both A and B   D. all of the above

12. When CAD is used for mechanical designs, _____ based graphics are   12._____
    preferred.
    A. raster   B. vector
    C. both A and B   D. all of the above

13. CAD is also used in industrial   13._____
    A. aerospace   B. automotives
    C. shipbuilding   D. all of the above

14. Animations can also be created by using   14._____
    A. Photoshop   B. CAD
    C. Flash   D. all of the above

15. Photo simulations are prepared by using   15._____
    A. Photoshop   B. CAD
    C. CAAD   D. both A and B

16. 3D wireframe is an extension of _____ drafting.   16._____
    A. 2D   B. 3D
    C. linear   D. all of the above

17. AutoCAD software for 2D drafting provides   17._____
    A. customization   B. quick design
    C. precise templates   D. all of the above

18. _____ is concerned with design blueprints.   18._____
    A. CAD pro technical drawing B. Softimage
    C. Edraw   D. None of the above

19. Speed, efficiency, and portability are benefits of   19._____
    A. AutoCAD   B. CAD pro technical drawing
    C. both A and B   D. none of the above

20. Detailed technical drawings always save   20._____
    A. time   B. cost
    C. both A and B   D. none of the above

21. Engineers and designers mostly use _____ to create 3D models.   21._____
    A. Solid Edge 2D Drafting   B. Blender
    C. BRL-CAD   D. none of the above

22. The most famous 2D CAD software is
    A. FreeCAD
    B. Photoshop
    C. AutoCAD
    D. all of the above

    22._____

23. K3DSurf is used to draw
    A. mathematic models
    B. engineering
    C. architectural
    D. all of the above

    23._____

24. Graphic technician concerns _____ to prepare designs.
    A. graphic designer
    B. technical persons
    C. team leaders
    D. all of the above

    24._____

25. Patent designs are BEST handled by
    A. AutoCAD
    B. CAD Pro
    C. Blender
    D. all of the above

    25._____

KEY (CORRECT ANSWERS)

1. D		11. A	
2. B		12. B	
3. D		13. D	
4. C		14. D	
5. A		15. B	
6. B		16. A	
7. C		17. D	
8. D		18. A	
9. D		19. B	
10. A		20. C	

21. A
22. C
23. A
24. D
25. B

EXAMINATION SECTION
TEST 1

DIRECTIONS: Each question or incomplete statement is followed by several suggested answers or completions. Select the one that BEST answers the question or completes the statement. *PRINT THE LETTER OF THE CORRECT ANSWER IN THE SPACE AT THE RIGHT.*

1. The soil with the lowest bearing power is USUALLY

    A. clay   B. sand   C. peat   D. gravel

2. The PRIMARY reason for providing manholes in a sewer is to

    A. facilitate construction
    B. facilitate inspection and repairs
    C. minimize settlement
    D. aid in locating final street grades

3. The joint on cast iron soil pipe is GENERALLY

    A. tongue and groove   B. flanged
    C. bell and spigot   D. a Dresser coupling

4. The aggregate in wall plaster is USUALLY

    A. gypsum   B. cement   C. gravel   D. sand

Questions 5-8.

DIRECTIONS: Questions 5 to 8 inclusive refer to the diagram below.

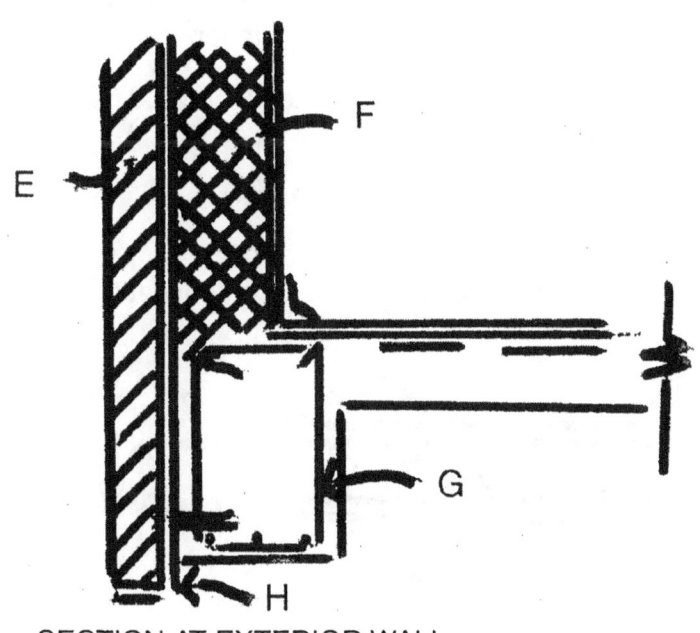

SECTION AT EXTERIOR WALL

5. The floor is made of 5.___

   A. air entrained concrete
   B. lightweight concrete
   C. plain concrete encased structural steel
   D. reinforced concrete

6. The member marked G is made of 6.___

   A. steel   B. galvanized wire
   C. copper   D. felt

7. The angle marked H is located 7.___

   A. at the bottom of a window
   B. at the top of a window
   C. at the side of a window
   D. along the window mullion

8. The letter E MOST LIKELY indicates 8.___

   A. architectural terra cotta   B. aluminum veneer
   C. brick   D. concrete masonry

9. Brick walls are occasionally washed down with a weak solution of muriatic acid. The chemical formula for muriatic acid is 9.___

   A. H_2SO_4 B. NH_4OH C. HNO_3 D. HCl

10. Based upon the manner in which the load is supported in a building structure, a joist is akin to a 10.___

    A. beam   B. column   C. rafter   D. stud

11. The vertical wood members in the walls of a one story wood frame residence are called 11.___

    A. sills   B. sleepers   C. headers   D. studs

Questions 12-13.

DIRECTIONS: Questions 12 and 13 refer to the part of foundation wall and support.

PLAN

12. The thickness of the wall is indicated by letter 12.___

    A. E   B. F   C. G   D. H

13. The item indicated by letter K is a   13._____
    A. door   B. vent   C. inset   D. window

14. The element when added to steel that will give the steel high strength and toughness is   14._____
    A. magnesium   B. manganese
    C. phosphorus   D. sulphur

15. Of the following species of lumber, the one that is NOT considered a hardwood is   15._____
    A. maple   B. oak   C. pine   D. birch

16. A carrying scraper would MOST LIKELY be employed on a   16._____
    A. sewer project
    B. building foundation excavation
    C. highway project
    D. tunnel project

17. Color is USUALLY imparted to a paint by the   17._____
    A. extender   B. thinner   C. retarder   D. pigment

18. A hip rafter in a wood frame building would MOST LIKELY be found in the   18._____
    A. foundation   B. walls   C. floors   D. roof

19. It is specified that the steel framework for the addition to an existing hospital building 19._____
    shall be all welded. Of the following, the BEST reason for this requirement is that welding
    A. is easier to perform in the field than riveting
    B. produces a more rigid structure than riveting
    C. is quieter than riveting
    D. is a more flexible method, when tieing into an existing structure

20. A sheet asphalt pavement in the City consists of a 6 inch layer of concrete, a 1½ inch   20._____
    layer of sheet asphalt and a 1½ inch layer of coarse graded asphalt binder course. The
    order in which these layers will occur when in place is
    A. concrete layer on top, binder course in the middle and sheet asphalt layer on the bottom
    B. sheet asphalt layer on top, concrete layer in the middle and binder course on bottom
    C. sheet asphalt layer on top, binder course in the middle and concrete layer on the bottom
    D. binder course on top, sheet asphalt layer in the middle and concrete layer on the bottom

KEY (CORRECT ANSWERS)

1. C
2. B
3. C
4. D
5. D

6. A
7. B
8. C
9. D
10. A

11. D
12. A
13. D
14. B
15. C

16. C
17. D
18. D
19. C
20. C

TEST 2

DIRECTIONS: Each question or incomplete statement is followed by several suggested answers or completions. Select the one that BEST answers the question or completes the statement. *PRINT THE LETTER OF THE CORRECT ANSWER IN THE SPACE AT THE RIGHT.*

1. The expression $\sqrt{7} + \sqrt{28}$ reduces to

   A. $3\sqrt{7}$ B. $\sqrt{35}$ C. $\sqrt{196}$ D. 7 3/2

   1.____

2. $(1 + r)^4$ is equal to

   A. $1 + 3r + 6r^2 + 3r^3 + r^4$ B. $1 + 2r + 3r^2 + 2r^3 + r^4$
   C. $1 + 4r + 6r^2 + 4r^3 + r^4$ D. $1 + 6r + 12r^2 + 6r^3 + r^4$

   2.____

3. Which of the following is a root in the equation $3x^3 + 8x^2 + 9x + 10 = 0$?

   A. -5   B. -4   C. -3   D. -2

   3.____

4. The curve of the equation $y = 3x^2 + 2$

   A. crosses the x axis 3 times
   B. crosses the x axis twice
   C. does not cross the x axis
   D. crosses the x axis once

   4.____

5. When C is greater than zero the equation $xy = C$ would plot MOST NEARLY as in

   5.____

   A.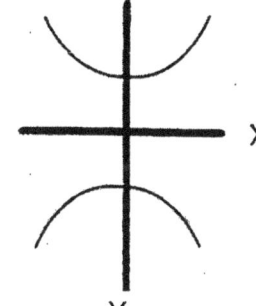
   B.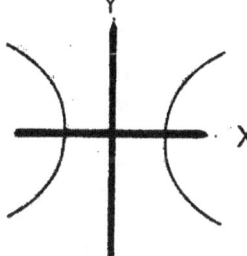
   C.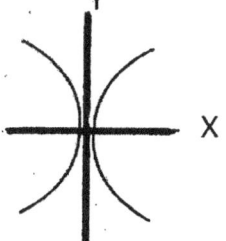
   D.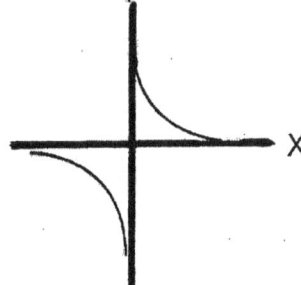

2 (#2)

6. If $r = \sqrt{\dfrac{I}{A}}$ then I equals

   A. $r^2 - A$
   B. $\sqrt{rA}$
   C. $r^2 A^2$
   D. $r^2 A$

7. If the sum of the squares of the two legs of a right triangle is 230,000 square feet, then the length of the hypotenuse is, in feet, MOST NEARLY,

   A. 480
   B. 365
   C. 570
   D. 1130

8. If $x = \sqrt{.62y^2}$ then $x^2 =$

   A. $.8y$
   B. $.64y^2$
   C. $\sqrt{.8Y}$
   D. $.8\sqrt{Y}$

9. If $x = \sqrt{p-r}$ then $x =$

   A. $\dfrac{1}{(P-r)^2}$
   B. $\dfrac{1}{P-r}$
   C. $(P-r)^{\frac{1}{2}}$
   D. $\sqrt{P} - \sqrt{r}$

10. The reciprocal of $\dfrac{2p}{5r}$ is

    A. $-\dfrac{2P}{5P}$
    B. $\sqrt{\dfrac{2P}{5r}}$
    C. $\dfrac{5r}{2P}$
    D. $10\,Pr$

11. $(7x - 2y)(3x + 9y) =$

    A. $21x^2 + 57xy - 18y^2$
    B. $21x^2 + 11xy - 18y^2$
    C. $10x^2 + 11xy + 7y^2$
    D. $7x^2 + 19xy - 6y^2$

12. If the $\cos(x + y) = \cos x \cos y - \sin x \sin y$, the $\cos 2g$ is equal to

    A. $2 \cos 2g$
    B. $\cos g \cos x - \sin g \sin x$
    C. $\cos g \cos x - \sin g \sin x$
    D. $\cos^2 g - \sin 2g$

13. The length of curved curb shown below is, in feet, MOST NEARLY,

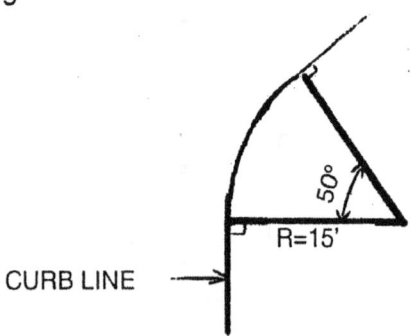

    A. 12.6
    B. 13.1
    C. 13.6
    D. 14.1

14. In the triangle shown below, the length of line EF is, MOST NEARLY,

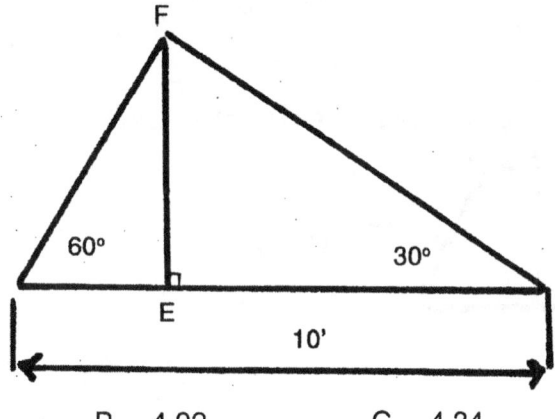

A. 4.00   B. 4.22   C. 4.34   D. 5.00

15. The area of the shaded figure shown below is, MOST NEARLY,

A. $.16D^2$ B. $.21D^2$ C. $.25D^2$ D. $.27D^2$

16. The area of the shaded figure shown below is, in square feet, MOST NEARLY,

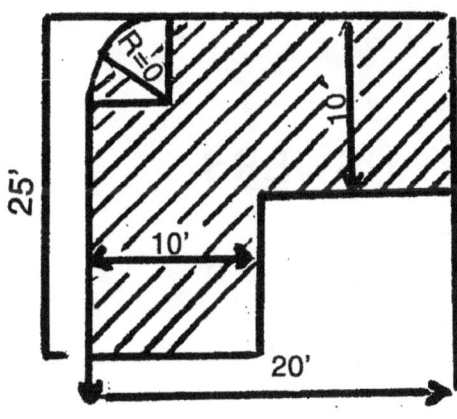

A. 342   B. 345   C. 348   D. 351

17. If $Y = X^{2X}$, the value of Y for X = 3 is

A. 27   B. 81   C. 243   D. 729

18. The equation $3X^3 - 5X^2 - 15X - 1 = y$ will cross the X axis for values of X between

A. X = 0 and X = 1
C. X = 2 and X = 3
B. X = 1 and X = 2
D. X = 3 and X = 4

4 (#2)

19. The shape of the surface created by a plane cutting the right cone as shown below would be   19.___

A. a parabola
C. an ellipse
B. a hyperbola
D. a circle

20. The area of the shaded part of the circle shown below is, MOST NEARLY,   20.___

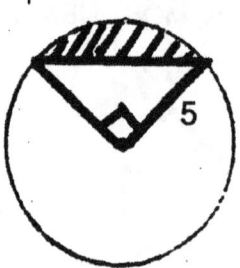

A. 6.1   B. 7.1   C. 8.1   D. 9.1

KEY (CORRECT ANSWERS)

1. A
2. C
3. D
4. C
5. D
6. D
7. A
8. B
9. C
10. C

11. A
12. D
13. B
14. C
15. B
16. A
17. D
18. D
19. C
20. B

TEST 3

DIRECTIONS: Each question or incomplete statement is followed by several suggested answers or completions. Select the one that BEST answers the question or completes the statement. *PRINT THE LETTER OF THE CORRECT ANSWER IN THE SPACE AT THE RIGHT.*

Questions 1-3.

DIRECTIONS: Questions 1 through 3 inclusive refer to the levelling notes below.

STa	BS	HI	FS	Elev.
BM1	7.11			716.22
TP1	8.72		6.91	
TP2	11.61		8.15	
BM2			9.25	

1. The elevation of TP1 is

   A. 717.02   B. 730.24   C. 723.33   D. 716.42

2. The elevation of BM2 is

   A. 719.35   B. 725.57   C. 716.99   D. 718.42

3. The elevation of the HI between TP1 and TP2 is

   A. 723.33   B. 725.14   C. 728.60   D. 707.30

KEY (CORRECT ANSWERS)

1. D
2. A
3. B

TEST 4

DIRECTIONS: Each question or incomplete statement is followed by several suggested answers or completions. Select the one that BEST answers the question or completes the statement. *PRINT THE LETTER OF THE CORRECT ANSWER IN THE SPACE AT THE RIGHT.*

1. A micrometer is USUALLY used to   1.___

   A. measure an outside diameter
   B. measure the distance between two points on a plank surface
   C. check a class of thread
   D. determine the center of a circle

2. A bolt is designated as 1/2 - 13 NC 2 X 1 3/4. The 1/2 means MOST NEARLY   2.___

   A. class of fit   B. length of bolt
   C. diameter   D. 100,000 pounds

3. A "kip" equals   3.___

   A. 100 pounds   B. 1000 pounds
   C. 10,000 pounds   D. 100,000 pounds

4. The operation of threading a drilled hole is called   4.___

   A. lapping   B. reaming
   C. breaching   D. tapping

5. A scale of 1/120 is the same as a scale of   5.___

   A. 1/8 inch equals a foot
   B. 1 inch equals 10 feet
   C. 3/16 inch equals 1 foot
   D. 1 inch equals 12 feet

6. Seasoning lumber is the drying out of the moisture that is normally present in green lumber. Of the following, the BEST reason for specifying seasoned lumber for floor beams is that   6.___

   A. seasoned lumber will not warp as much as unseasoned lumber
   B. it is easier to paint seasoned lumber
   C. it is easier to drive nails into seasoned lumber
   D. seasoned lumber weighs less thereby reducing shipping costs

7. Turning of metals is USUALLY performed on a   7.___

   A. radial drill press   B. lathe
   C. milling machine   D. shaper

8. Of the following, the BEST reason for using lightweight aggregate for plastering a wall is   8.___

   A. the dead load will be reduced
   B. lightweight aggregate produces a finer finish
   C. lightweight aggregate is less expensive than ordinary aggregate
   D. you can substitute 2-coat plaster with lightweight aggregate in place of 3-coat plaster with ordinary aggregate

9. The property of steel that makes it suitable for use in a cable is its strength in 9.____

   A. compression   B. tension   C. shear   D. torsion

10. A specification for steel erection prohibits the use of heat in straightening material that was bent in shipment. Of the following, the BEST reason for this requirement is that heating the steel may 10.____

    A. ruin the shop coat of paint
    B. warp the piece thereby making it difficult to fit in place
    C. injure the strength of the steel
    D. necessitate the use of special equipment thereby increasing the cost of the job

11. Quoting from the specifications, "Approved sheepsfoot rollers shall be used for compacting all parts of the embankment which they can reach," the above quotation MOST likely refers to the construction of a(n) 11.____

    A. skyscraper   B. large monolithic sewer
    C. earth dam   D. aqueduct

12. Which is the MOST restrictive traffic sign? 12.____

    A. No Stopping   B. No Standing
    C. No Parking   D. Bus Stop

13. Of the following, the coating that should be placed on wood to preserve the lumber and reveal the grain and texture of the material is 13.____

    A. enamel   B. varnish
    C. rubber base paint   D. turpentine

14. Water distribution mains 6" in diameter and larger are USUALLY made of 14.____

    A. cast iron   B. steel   C. concrete   D. clay

15. In the recent past there was a controversy concerning the addition of a chemical to our water supply system. The chemical in question was 15.____

    A. chlorine   B. alum   C. copper sulfate   D. fluorine

16. The density of water is a maximum when its temperature is, in degrees centigrade, MOST NEARLY, 16.____

    A. 4   B. 0   C. 100   D. 32

17. A meter is, in inches, MOST NEARLY 17.____

    A. 39.4   B. 46.2   C. 50.0   D. 100.0

18. Another name for the North Star is 18.____

    A. Vega   B. Polaris   C. Altair   D. Argo

19. A pictorial drawing, two of the axes of which are 30° with the horizontal, is known as a(n) 19.____

    A. diametric drawing   B. isometric drawing
    C. perspective drawing   D. oblique drawing

20. Of the five items following, how many bear a close relationship to each other?   20._____
    1. pile loading test
    2. needle
    3. underpinning
    4. pretest pile
    5. shore

    A. all   B. four   C. three   D. two

KEY (CORRECT ANSWERS)

1. A   11. C
2. C   12. A
3. B   13. B
4. D   14. A
5. B   15. D

6. A   16. A
7. B   17. A
8. A   18. B
9. B   19. B
10. C   20. A

TEST 5

DIRECTIONS: Each question or incomplete statement is followed by several suggested answers or completions. Select the one that BEST answers the question or completes the statement. *PRINT THE LETTER OF THE CORRECT ANSWER IN THE SPACE AT THE RIGHT.*

1. The downward acceleration of a falling body is 32 feet per second per second. This means MOST NEARLY that the

   A. velocity changes 32 feet per second each second
   B. distance the body falls increases at rate of 32 feet per second
   C. the acceleration varies with time
   D. velocity is 32 feet per second

   1.____

2. The weight of a 2 cubic foot block is 300 pounds. The weight of this block when submerged in water, as shown below, would be, in pounds, MOST NEARLY

   A. 175   B. 362   C. 238   D. 424

   2.____

   Water weighs 62.5 #/cu.ft.

3. The specific gravity of a liquid is 0.5. This means MOST NEARLY that the

   A. weight of the liquid is approximately 31 pounds per cubic foot
   B. mass of the liquid is 0.5g
   C. liquid is heavier than water
   D. density of the liquid is 0.5

   3.____

4. The ph value of a liquid will indicate

   A. the specific gravity of the liquid
   B. the degree of pollution of the liquid
   C. the dissolved oxygen content of the liquid
   D. whether the liquid is acid or base

   4.____

5. A B.T.U.(British Thermal Unit) is a unit of

   A. force   B. energy   C. power   D. temperature

   5.____

6. Of the following chemicals, the one that is MOST commonly used in a water supply system to destroy harmful bacteria is

   A. fluorine   B. chlorine   C. bromine   D. iodine

   6.____

7. An automobile moving 30 miles per hour is moving MOST NEARLY

   A. 30 feet per second   B. 35 feet per second
   C. 45 feet per second   D. 40 feet per second

   7.____

33

8. The fact that one may have a free surface while the other may not, distinguishes between a

   A. fluid and a gas
   B. fluid and a liquid
   C. solid and a fluid
   D. liquid and a gas

9. The smallest unit of a chemical compound that retains the characteristic of the compound is USUALLY a(n)

   A. neutron   B. atom   C. proton   D. molecule

10. Electricity is sometimes compared to the flow of water. Pressure of water is equivalent to which of the following terms in electricity?

    A. current
    B. voltage
    C. resistance
    D. conductivity

11. Which of the following is a unit of electrical power?

    A. ohm   B. watt   C. volt   D. kilowatt hour

12. Electric light bulbs are USUALLY rated in

    A. amperes   B. watts   C. henries   D. ohms

13. Which of the following pieces of electrical equipment would be used to change 660 volts AC current to 110 volts AC current?

    A. rectifier
    B. condenser
    C. transformer
    D. converter

14. The machining operation of cutting a keyway inside a drilled hole is known as

    A. reaming
    B. broaching
    C. boring
    D. tapping

15. Ozone is a form of

    A. oxygen
    B. notrigen
    C. chlorine
    D. zinc oxide

16. Of the following, the primary element in MOST fertilizers is

    A. carbon   B. aluminum   C. nitrogen   D. iron

17. Salt thrown in icy pavements MAINLY

    A. provides an abrasive material that will grip the ice
    B. lowers the freezing temperature of the water
    C. breaks the bond between the ice and the pavement
    D. ionizes the ice crystals

18. Of the following elements, the one MOST commonly found in clay is

    A. fluorine
    B. aluminum
    C. carbon
    D. iron

19. In the equation F = ma, "a" can be expressed in which of the following units? 19._____

    A. $\dfrac{Ft}{Sec^2}$
    B. miles per hour
    C. poundals
    D. kilograms/cm^2

20. The force "F" required to lift the 200# load with the lever shown in the sketch below is, in pounds, MOST NEARLY 20._____

    A. 60   B. 120   C. 100   D. 80

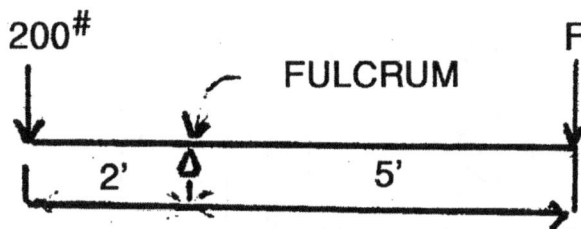

KEY (CORRECT ANSWERS)

1.	A	11.	B
2.	A	12.	B
3.	A	13.	C
4.	D	14.	B
5.	D	15.	A
6.	B	16.	C
7.	C	17.	B
8.	C	18.	B
9.	D	19.	A
10.	B	20.	D

TEST 6

DIRECTIONS: Each question or incomplete statement is followed by several suggested answers or completions. Select the one that BEST answers the question or completes the statement. *PRINT THE LETTER OF THE CORRECT ANSWER IN THE SPACE AT THE RIGHT.*

Questions 1-5.

DIRECTIONS: Questions 1 through 5 inclusive, refer to the diagram shown below.

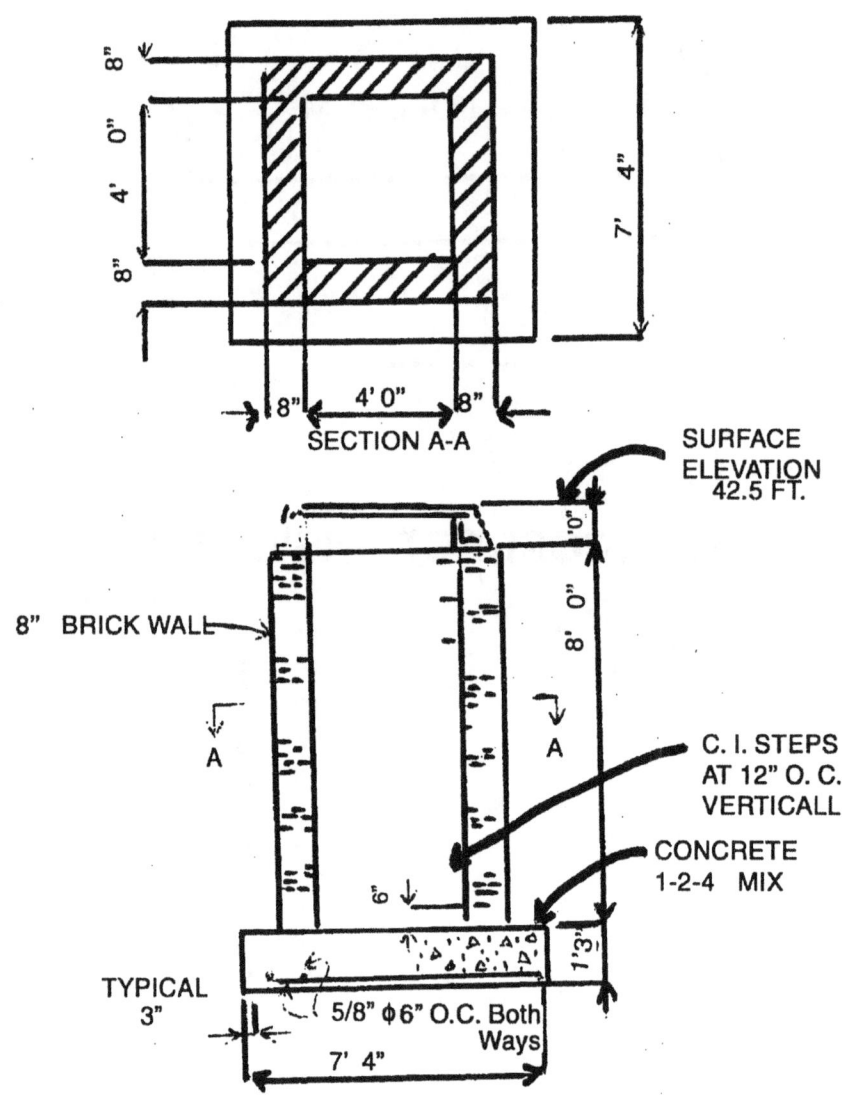

1. The volume of concrete in the base of the manhole is, in cubic feet, MOST NEARLY,   1.___
   A. 56   B. 61   C. 63   D. 67

2. The elevation of the bottom of the concrete base of the manhole is, in feet   2.___
   A. 32.25   B. 32.50'   C. 52.75   D. 41.5

3. If 21 brick are required for a cubic foot of brick wall, the number of brick required to build the manhole walls is, MOST NEARLY,

   A. 100   B. 1500   C. 1800   D. 2100

4. The length of a typical 5/8 round bar in the concrete base is

   A. 6'10"   B. 7'0"   C. 7'2"   D. 7'4"

5. The number of cast iron steps required for the brick wall is, MOST NEARLY,

   A. 6   B. 7   C. 8   D. 9

KEY (CORRECT ANSWERS)

1. D

2. A

3. D

4. A

5. C

TEST 7

DIRECTIONS: Each question or incomplete statement is followed by several suggested answers or completions. Select the one that BEST answers the question or completes the statement. *PRINT THE LETTER OF THE CORRECT ANSWER IN THE SPACE AT THE RIGHT.*

1. The volume of the solid shown below is, MOST NEARLY, 1.____

   A. 64 B. 32 C. $32\sqrt{2}$ D. $16\sqrt{2}$

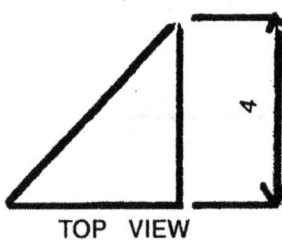

TOP VIEW

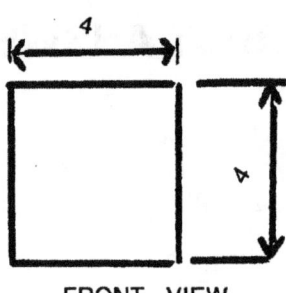

FRONT VIEW

2. The volume of the solid shown below is, MOST NEARLY 2.____

   A. 200 B. 220 C. 240 D. 260

TOP VIEW

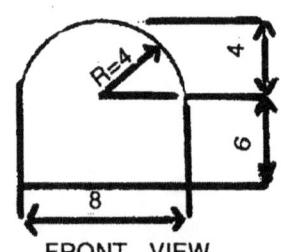

FRONT VIEW

3. In the front view of the block shown below, the V refers to the 3.____
   A. class of fit
   B. finish on that surface
   C. type of knurl to be machined on that surface
   D. class of steel to be used for the block

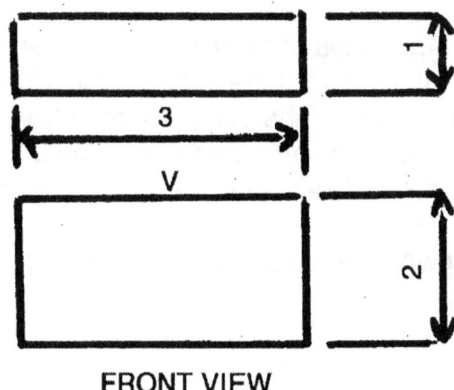

FRONT VIEW

KEY (CORRECT ANSWERS)

1. B

2. B

3. B

TEST 8

DIRECTIONS: Each question or incomplete statement is followed by several suggested answers or completions. Select the one that BEST answers the question or completes the statement. *PRINT THE LETTER OF THE CORRECT ANSWER IN THE SPACE AT THE RIGHT.*

Questions 1-10.

DIRECTIONS: In each of the following groups of drawings the top view and front elevation of an object are shown at the left. At the right are four drawings, one of which represents the end elevation of the object as seen from the right. Select the drawing which represents the correct end elevation and mark the answer sheet with the letter of this drawing on line with the number of the question.

The first group is shown as an example only. The correct answer is c.

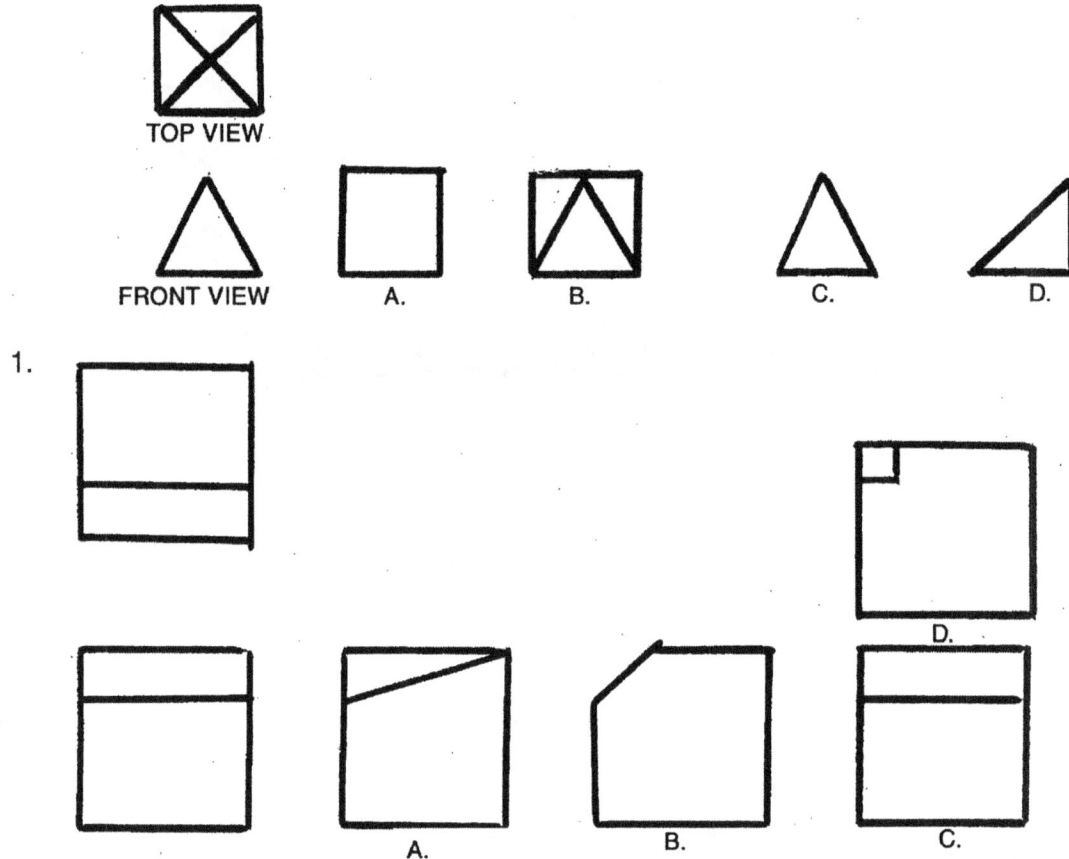

1.   1.___

40

2 (#8)

2.

2.____

A.   B.   C.   D.

3.

3.____

A.   B.   C.   D.

4.

4.____

A.   B.   C.   D.

5.

5.____

A.   B.   C.   D.

41

6. 6.____

7. 7.____

8. 8.____

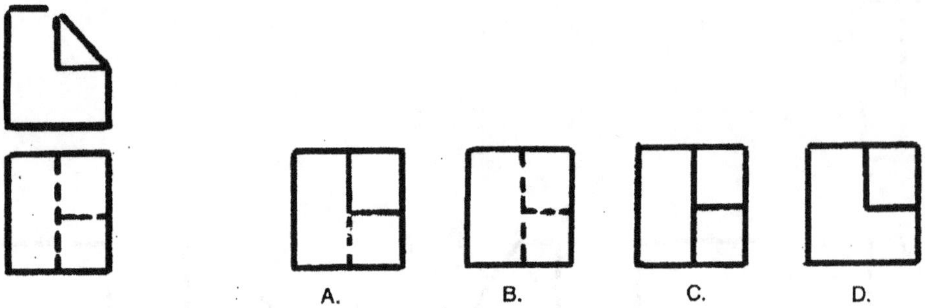

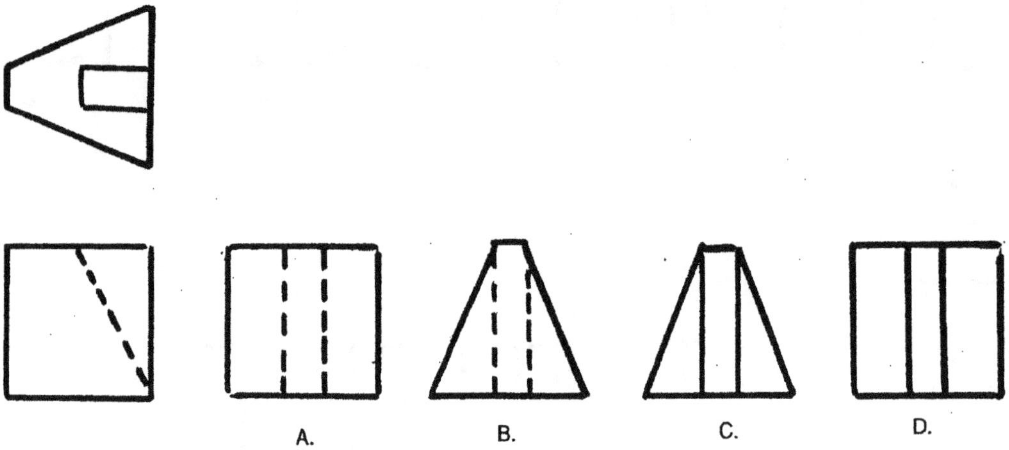

9. The volume of the solid shown below is MOST NEARLY 9.____

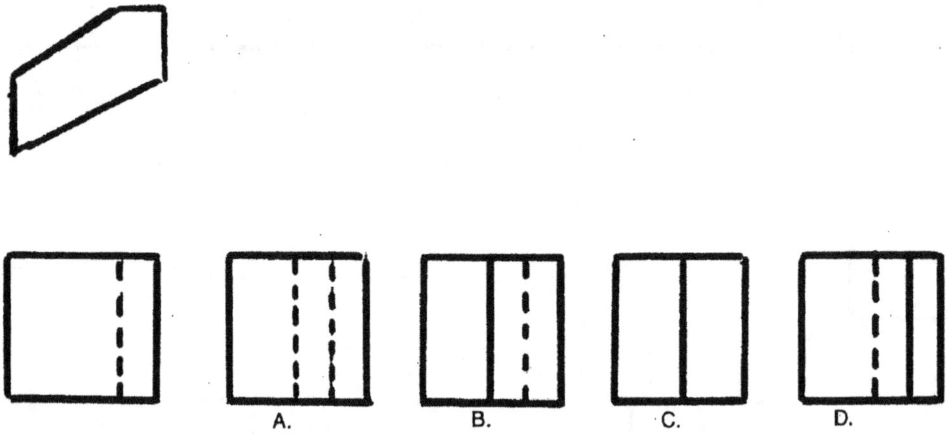

A. 264 B. 272 C. 280 D. 288

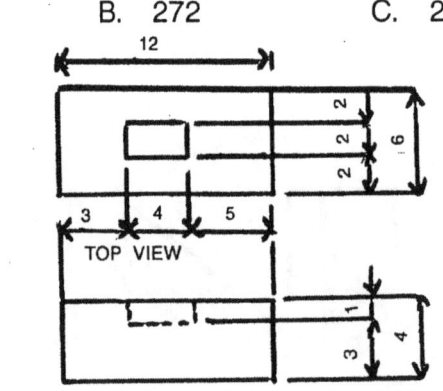

10. The volume of the solid shown below is, MOST NEARLY, 10.____

    A. $275\sqrt{3}$ B. $275\sqrt{2}$ C. 350   D. $750\sqrt{3}$

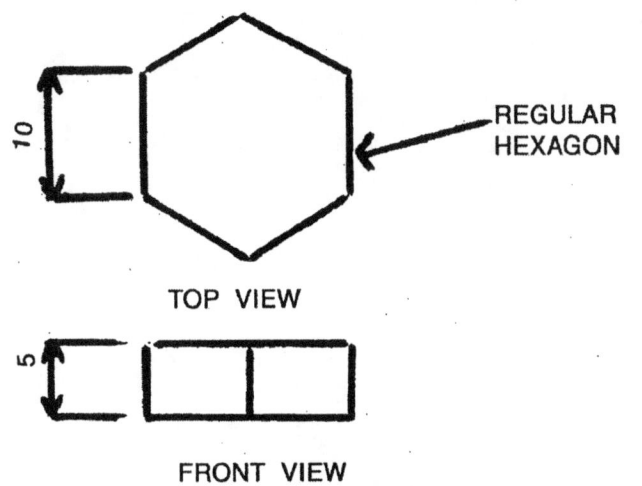

TOP VIEW

FRONT VIEW

KEY (CORRECT ANSWERS)

1. B   6. C
2. D   7. C
3. A   8. D
4. D   9. C
5. A   10. D

44

EXAMINATION SECTION
TEST 1

DIRECTIONS: Each question or incomplete statement is followed by several suggested answers or completions. Select the one that BEST answers the question or completes the statement. *PRINT THE LETTER OF THE CORRECT ANSWER IN THE SPACE AT THE RIGHT.*

1. A planimeter is an instrument used to measure

   A. areas B. angles C. distances D. elevations

2. In structural steel details, a line passing through the center of a row of rivets is called a(n) _____ line.

   A. section B. extension C. gage D. cut

3. In topographic maps, the lines drawn to show relief by means of hill shading are called

   A. hachures B. soundings C. grid lines D. flats

4. The projection of a circular cross-section, such as on a casting or forging, is called a

   A. bore B. chamfer C. core D. boss

5. On a diagrammatic piping drawing, the symbol USUALLY indicates a

   A. check valve
   C. cross
   B. union
   D. 90 elbow

6. The welding symbol USUALLY indicates a _____ weld.

   A. bead B. plug C. fillet D. groove

7. On an electrical wiring diagram, the symbol USUALLY indicates a

   A. junction box
   C. power panel
   B. ceiling outlet
   D. convenience outlet

8. A map is drawn to a scale of 1" = two miles. The distance between two points on the map is 2 1/2".
   The ACTUAL distance between the same two points on the ground is MOST NEARLY _____ feet.

   A. 25,200 B. 25,800 C. 26,400 D. 30,000

9. A topographic map is drawn to a scale of 1" = 200', with a contour interval of 2 feet. On a slope of 10%, the distance on the map between contours is MOST NEARLY _____ inches.

   A. 0.20 B. 0.15 C. 0.10 D. 0.05

10. The profile of a sewer is drawn to a scale of 1" = 50' Horizontal and 1" = 10' Vertical. The invert of the sewer drops 1.200 feet in a horizontal distance of 250 feet. The actual slope of the sewer is MOST NEARLY

   A. 0.40% B. 0.48% C. 0.54% D. 0.60%

10.____

11. When graph paper with logarithmically spaced rulings in both directions is used, an equation in which K and N are constants will plot as a straight line if it is of the form

   A. $y = \dfrac{K}{\log X} + \log N$ B. $y = KX^N$
   C. $y = K(\log X) + N$ D. $y = N(\log X) + K$

11.____

12. The distance between two trusses or transverse bents in a building is USUALLY called a

   A. set back B. story C. bay D. chase

12.____

13. The CORRECT right side view of the object whose top and front views are as shown on the right is

13.____

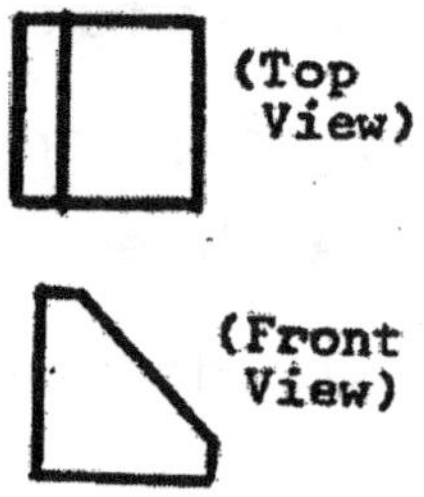

14. The CORRECT right side view of the object whose top and front views are as shown on the right is

14.____

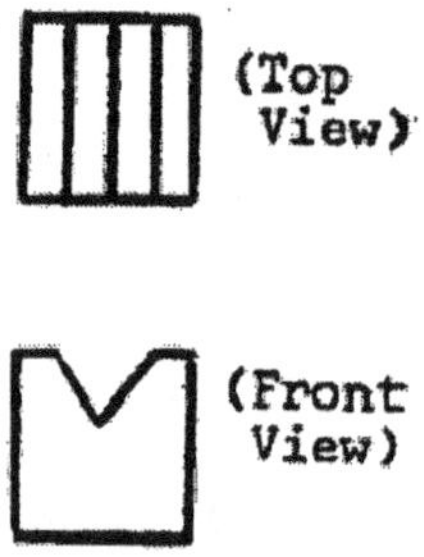

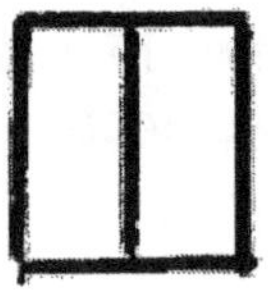

15. The CORRECT right side view of the object whose top and front views are as shown on the right is

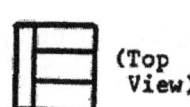 (Top View)

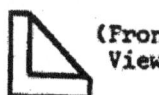 (Front View)

A.  B.  C.  D.

16. The CORRECT right side view of the object whose top and front views are as shown on the right is

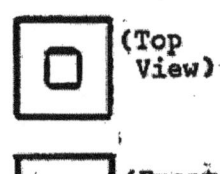

A.  B.  C.  D.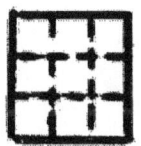

17. The expression $\left(\dfrac{T^6}{27}\right)^{1/3}$ is equivalent to

A. $\dfrac{T^2}{3}$ B. $\dfrac{T^{2/3}}{9}$ C. $\dfrac{T^{18}}{3}$ D. $\dfrac{T^{1/2}}{9}$

18. The fraction $\dfrac{\left(R - \dfrac{R}{t}\right)}{\left(\dfrac{1}{t}\right) - 1}$ is equal to

A. R   B. 1/R   C. -R   D. -Rt

19. In triangle ABC, $\beta = 8$, a = 9, and C = 135. The area of triangle ABC is

    A. 36 B. 30 C. $36\sqrt{2}$ D. $18\sqrt{2}$

19.____

20. Function y varies inversely as x. If y = 1 when x = 9, then when x = 3, y is equal to

    A. 2 B. 3 C. 12 D. 18

20.____

KEY (CORRECT ANSWERS)

1. A   11. B
2. C   12. C
3. A   13. B
4. D   14. D
5. A   15. A

6. C   16. C
7. D   17. A
8. C   18. C
9. C   19. D
10. B   20. B

TEST 2

DIRECTIONS: Each question or incomplete statement is followed by several suggested answers or completions. Select the one that BEST answers the question or completes the statement. *PRINT THE LETTER OF THE CORRECT ANSWER IN THE SPACE AT THE RIGHT.*

1. If the product of 0.02 and 0.0003 is written in the form 6×10^n, the value of n is 1.____
   A. -3 B. -4 C. -5 D. -6

2. The value of $\sqrt{275.56}$ is 2.____
   A. 15.8 B. 16.2 C. 16.6 D. 16.9

3. The sum of the interior angles of a polygon is 1620. The number of sides of the polygon is 3.____
   A. 9 B. 10 C. 11 D. 12

4. The angles of a triangle are in the ratio of 3:5:7. The number of degrees in the SMALLEST angle of the triangle is 4.____
   A. 24 B. 30 C. 36 D. 45

5. The line $2y = 6x + 4$ intersects the x axis at 5.____
   A. 2 B. 3/2 C. -1/2 D. -2/3

6. The cosine of 210° is 6.____
   A. $\frac{1}{2}$ B. $\frac{\sqrt{3}}{2}$ C. $\frac{-\sqrt{3}}{2}$ D. $\frac{-\sqrt{1}}{2}$

7. The coordinates of point A are (-3,-2) and the coordinates of point B are (2,10). The length of line AB is 7.____
   A. 18 B. 13 C. 10 D. 6

8. In the function $y = 4x^3 - 2x^2 + x^{-1}$, when $x = -2$, the value of y is 8.____
   A. 40 1/2 B. 24 1/2 C. -6 1/2 D. -40 1/2

9. The number of degrees in 1.5π radians is 9.____
   A. A.300 B. B.270 C. C.240 D. D.180

10. f $\log_{10} y = 3$, y equals 10.____
    A. 2.718 B. 100 C. 1000 D. 1122

11. One angle of a right angle triangle is 45°. If the perimeter is 16, the length of the hypotenuse is MOST NEARLY 11.____
    A. 5.42 B. 6.63 C. 7.89 D. 12.50

12. The expression (10a² - 3a - 18) divided by (5a+6) is equal to   12._____

    A. (2a+3)   B. (3a-2)   C. (3a+2)   D. (2a-3)

13. A 2" x 10" wood joist is horizontal and spans 12 feet. If the 10" side is vertical, the   13._____
    moment of inertia of the joist about a horizontal axis through the center of gravity is
    MOST NEARLY

    A. 137"⁴   B. 167"⁴   C. 197"⁴   D. 227"⁴

14. he rate o| flow over a weir is given by the formula $Q = 3.33bh^{3/2}$. When b = 10 and h = 4,   14._____
    the rate of flow, Q, is MOST NEARLY

    A. 234   B. 240   C. 252   D. 266

15. A concrete sidewalk 6 feet wide is to be constructed around a circular swimming pool.   15._____
    If the inside diameter of the sidewalk is 50 feet, the surface area of the sidewalk is
    MOST NEARLY

    A. 955 ft.²   B. 1055 ft.²   C. 1155 ft²   D. 1255 ft.²

16. A horizontal board 10 feet long is supported at each end. When a man stands on the   16._____
    board 3 feet from the right support, the right reaction, neglecting the weight of the board,
    is 140 pounds.
    If this man stood at the center of the board, the right reaction, neglecting the weight of
    the board, would be pounds.

    A. 120   B. 110   C. 100   D. 90

17. Water flows through an 8 inch diameter pipe at the rate of 1000 gpm. If 7.48 gals = 1   17._____
    cu.ft., the average velocity in the pipe is _____ ft./sec.

    A. 9.11   B. 8.02   C. 7.41   D. 6.39

18. A concrete retaining wall is 150 feet long and 12 feet high. The cross-section is trapezoi-   18._____
    dal with a base of 24 inches and a top width of 12 inches.
    The volume of the wall is MOST NEARLY _____ cubic yards.

    A. 90   B. 100   C. 110   D. 120

19. A cantilever beam 12 feet long carries a uniformly distributed load of 300 pounds per foot   19._____
    including the weight of the beam.
    The bending moment at the support is _____ foot/pounds.

    A. 18400   B. 20400   C. 21600   D. 22600

20. A shaft rotates at 120 rpm and delivers 20 horsepower.   20._____
    If 550 ft. lbs. per second .equals one horsepower, the torque in the shaft is MOST
    NEARLY _____ foot/pounds.

    A. 76   B. 80   C. 88   D. 94

KEY (CORRECT ANSWERS)

1. D
2. C
3. C
4. C
5. D

6. C
7. B
8. D
9. B
10. C

11. B
12. D
13. B
14. D
15. B

16. C
17. D
18. B
19. C
20. C

EXAMINATION SECTION
TEST 1

DIRECTIONS: Each question or incomplete statement is followed by several suggested answers or completions. Select the one that BEST answers the question or completes the statement. *PRINT THE LETTER OF THE CORRECT ANSWER IN THE SPACE AT THE RIGHT.*

1. An empty tank is 6 feet in diameter and 10 feet long. The tank is placed underground in a horizontal position and to a depth where the ground water level is 4 feet above the top of the tank.
   The buoyant force on the tank due to the ground water is MOST NEARLY _____ lbs.

   A. 15,600   B. 16,600   C. 17,600   D. 18,600

2. A wide flange steel beam has a moment of inertia about axis x-x of 3446.5 in.4 and a depth of 27.0 in.
   The section modulus is MOST NEARLY _____ in.^{3}

   A. 240   B. 255   C. 270   D. 285

3. A pump discharges 2 cfs of water weighing 62.4 pcf at a head of 30 feet.
   The output horsepower of the pump is MOST NEARLY _____ HP.

   A. 5.4   B. 6.0   C. 6.8   D. 7.6

4. Water flows through a 6" diameter orifice in the vertical side of a steel tank.
   If the head causing flow is 16 feet, the rate of flow, neglecting losses, is _____ cu.ft./sec.

   A. 6.30   B. 7,30   C. 8.30   D. 9.30

5. A one-inch diameter steel bar, 5 feet long, is subjected to a tensile force of 10,000 pounds.
   If the modulus of elasticity, E, is 30 x 10^6 psi, the elongation of the bar is _____ in.

   A. .015   B. .025   C. .035   D. .045

6. The charges for water are as follows:
   First 10,000 cu.ft. $3.00/1,000 cu.ft.
   Next 900,000 cu.ft. $2.00/1,000 cu.ft.
   If a customer receives a bill for $90, the quantity of water used is _____ cu.ft.

   A. 40,000   B. 42,000   C. 44,000   D. 46,000

7. The velocity in a 6-inch diameter water pipe is 10 feet per second.
   The velocity in an 8-inch diameter pipe carrying the same discharge is MOST NEARLY _____ ft./sec.

   A. 7.8   B. 13.3   C. 5.6   D. 4.2

8. *WYE-WYE* and *DELTA-WYE* are two

   A. types of D.C. motor windings
   B. types of electrical splices

C. arrangements of 3-phase transformer connections
D. shapes of electrical fuses

9. A beam supporting the masonry over an opening in a wall is a
   A. lintel B. soffit C. parapet D. jamb

10. Very small quantities of fatty acid materials or Vinsol resin are added during the manufacture of portland cement to produce _____ cement.
    A. high-early strength B. white portland
    C. air-entraining portland D. oil well

11. When finely divided sand is subjected to the lifting action of water flowing upward through its mass causing it to behave as a liquid, it is called
    A. loam B. gumbo C. peat D. quicksand

12. Wood piles are impregnated with creosote PRIMARILY to
    A. improve appearance B. prevent fires
    C. reduce decay D. increase conductivity

13. A method used for placing concrete under water is the _____ method.
    A. auger B. wellpoint C. needle D. tremie

14. A beam resting on the top chord of a roof truss and supporting the rafters or other roof construction is called a
    A. purlin B. spandrel
    C. lintel D. grade beam

15. A type of brick bond in which every sixth course of stretcher bond is made a header course is _____ bond.
    A. English B. Flemish C. common D. cross

16. The side member of a window or door opening is called a
    A. sill B. saddle C. head D. jamb

17. Wood members, 2 in. x 4 in., installed 16 inches on center in a wood-frame dwelling are called
    A. rafters B. sills C. joists D. studs

18. A concrete beam which is placed under initial stress by tensioning the steel wires comprising the reinforcement prior to its receiving any stress due to the dead or live load is called a
    A. eb joist B. prestressed beam
    C. plate girder D. laminated beam

19. Vermiculite is a lightweight aggregate which is mixed with gypsum to form a
    A. fire-resistant coating B. flashing
    C. membrane waterproofing D. non-expansion joint

20. When stucco is applied in three coats, the coats are usually called the finish coat, the   20._____
    brown coat, and the _____ coat.
    A. earth   B. sheathing   C. scratch   D. mullion

KEY (CORRECT ANSWERS)

1.	C	11.	D
2.	B	12.	C
3.	C	13.	D
4.	A	14.	A
5.	B	15.	C
6.	A	16.	D
7.	C	17.	D
8.	C	18.	B
9.	A	19.	A
10.	C	20.	C

TEST 2

DIRECTIONS: Each question or incomplete statement is followed by several suggested answers or completions. Select the one that BEST answers the question or completes the statement. *PRINT THE LETTER OF THE CORRECT ANSWER IN THE SPACE AT THE RIGHT.*

1. The angle between the *true* meridian and the *magnetic* meridian is called the

    A. zimuth B. bearing
    C. magnetic declination D. longitude

2. A scale of 1/24000 is the same as a scale of

    A. one-quarter inch equals one foot
    B. 1 inch equals 2000 feet
    C. 1 inch equals 1 mile
    D. 1 foot equals 5000 feet

Questions 3-4.

DIRECTIONS: Questions 3 and 4 refer to the following notes on surveying leveling.

STA.	B.S.	H.I.	F.S.	Elev.
BM1	6.42	124.66		
TE1	5.88		1.63	
BM2			10.20	

3. The elevation of BM1 is MOST NEARLY

    A. 111.82   B. 118.24   C. 122.46   D. 125.78

4. The elevation of BM2 is MOST NEARLY

    A. 136.71   B. 124.62   C. 118.71   D. 112.11

5. The bearing of line AE is N24°-30'E, and the bearing of line AG is S12-0'E. The angle EAG is

    A. 36°-30'   B. 53°-30'   C. 78°-00'   D. 143°-30'

6. A horizontal angle is measured four times by repetition using a transit. If the horizontal plate reads 181°29'44", the angle is

    A. 45°22'26"   B. 46°13'27"   C. 54°12'13"   D. 61°18'12"

7. The distance between two points on the ground was found to be 1246.22 feet when measured with a nominal 50 foot steel tape that was actually 49.95 feet long. The ACTUAL distance between the two points is _____ ft.

    A. 1244.67   B. 1245.22   C. 1247.22   D. 1248.14

8. An 8-inch diameter sewer is laid on a slope of 0.42% between two manholes 300 feet apart.
   If the invert elevation at the upper end is 126.42 feet, the invert elevation at the lower end is _____ ft.

   A. 126.01   B. 125.94   C. 125.36   D. 125.16

9. A temperature of 100 degrees Fahrenheit is MOST NEARLY equal to _____ degrees C.

   A. 32   B. B,38   C. 112   D. 212

10. A square tank 10 feet wide and 12 feet high is filled with water weighing 62.4 pounds per cubic foot.
    The horizontal hydrostatic force on one side of the box is MOST NEARLY _____ lbs.

    A. 40,000   B. 45,000   C. 50,000   D. 55,000

11. Dry ice is made from

    A. hydrogen sulfide   B. carbon dioxide
    C. calcium oxide   D. sodium chloride

12. The chemical symbol for silver is

    A. Ag   B. Au   C. Si   D. Se

13. Natural gas consists of *approximately* 90 percent

    A. chlorine   B. acetylene   C. oxygen   D. methane

14. Of the following, the instrument used to measure the specific gravity of the solution in an automobile battery is a(n)

    A. hygrometer   B. pyrometer
    C. hydrometer   D. radiometer

15. A circuit contains three 10-ohm resistors in series.
    The COMBINED equivalent resistance of the three resistors is _____ ohms.

    A. 1/30   B. 1/10   C. 10   D. 30

16. A car starting from rest accelerates at the rate of 8 ft./sec.^{2}
    At the end of 6 seconds, the car will have traveled a distance equal to _____ feet.

    A. 144   B. 136   C. 120   D. 94

17. A bag of cement estimated at 0.875 cubic foot of volume contains a net weight of cement equal to _____ lbs.

    A. 56   B. 78   C. 94   D. 112

18. The contractor shall regulate the consistency of the mix to the slump directed by the engineer.
    Such a statement is part of a specification for

    A. concrete   B. asphalt
    C. gravel   D. top soil

19. Mortar briquettes composed of one part of Portland cement and three parts of Standard Ottawa sand are USUALLY used for _____ strength tests.

    A. torsion
    B. compression
    C. impact
    D. tensile

20. The contractor shall submit to the engineer a CPM Construction Plan. In such a statement, CPM is an abbreviation for

    A. Control Path Method
    B. Critical Path Month
    C. Critical Path Method
    D. Control Per Month

KEY (CORRECT ANSWERS)

1. C
2. B
3. B
4. C
5. D
6. A
7. B
8. D
9. B
10. B
11. B
12. A
13. D
14. C
15. D
16. A
17. C
18. A
19. D
20. C

EXAMINATION SECTION
TEST 1

DIRECTIONS: Each question or incomplete statement is followed by several suggested answers or completions. Select the one that BEST answers the question or completes the statement. *PRINT THE LETTER OF THE CORRECT ANSWER IN THE SPACE AT THE RIGHT.*

1. A water pump delivers 250 g.p.m. at a head of 65 feet of water. If horsepower is equal to g.p.m. x h/3960, the horsepower delivered by this pump is MOST NEARLY 1.____

    A. 3.6 B. 4.1 C. 4.6 D. 5.1

2. In an electric circuit, if the voltage is 120 volts and the current is 15 amperes, the resistance, in ohms, is MOST NEARLY 2.____

    A. 1/8 B. 1 C. 4 D. 8

3. In the sketch shown at the right, R_R, in pounds, is MOST NEARLY 3.____
    A. 3200
    B. 3400
    C. 3500
    D. 3600

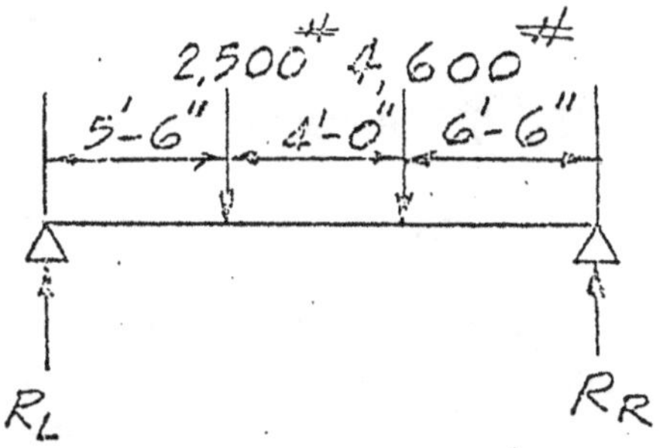

4. The volume of voids in a material is a measure of its 4.____

    A. viscosity B. porosity
    C. consistency D. ductility

5. The total resistance, in ohms, of the electric circuit in the sketch shown at the right is MOST NEARLY 5.____
    A. 11.3
    B. 14.5
    C. 17.2
    D. 23.0

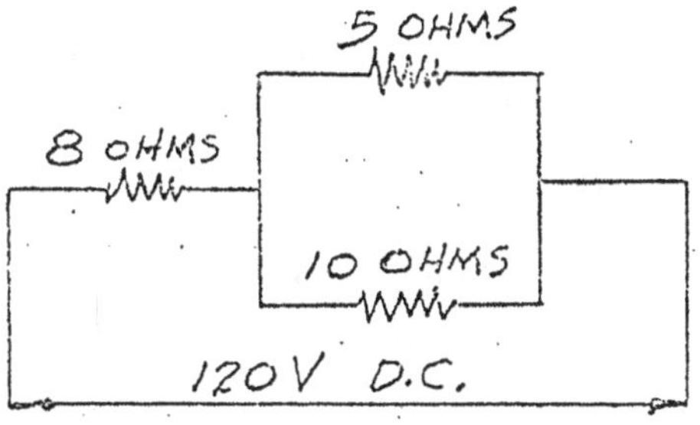

6. In addition to iron, which is the major component of ordinary structural steel, there are other chemical elements present. The element, other than iron, usually found in the greatest amount is 6.____

    A. carbon B. sulfur C. phosphorus D. boron

7.

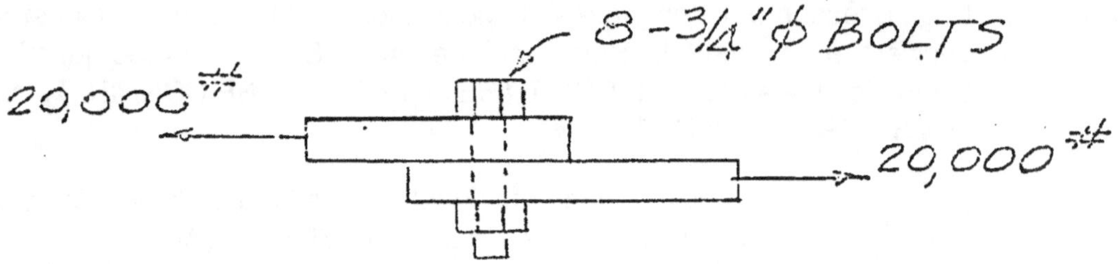

In the sketch shown above, the unit shearing stress in each bolt, in p.s.i., is MOST NEARLY

A. 3,600   B. 4,700   C. 5,700   D. 6,500

8. The $\log_{10} 100^6$ is MOST NEARLY

A. 6   B. 600   C. 12   D. 120

9. $(S\sqrt{-1})^2$ is equal to

A. $-25\sqrt{-1}$ B. $25\sqrt{-1}$ C. $+25$ D. -25

10. A square tract of land contains 57,600 square feet. The length of a fence needed to enclose the entire property is MOST NEARLY _____ feet.

A. 960   B. 752   C. 480   D. 300

11. If the weight of steel is 490 #/cu.ft., then the weight of a steel plate 6 ft. x 6 ft. x 1/4 inch is, in pounds, MOST NEARLY

A. 330   B. 370   C. 410   D. 450

12. The scale of a topographic map is 1 inch equals 60 feet. If 43,560 sq.ft. = 1 acre, the area of a rectangular tract of land that scales 21.5 inches by 42.3 inches is, in acres, MOST NEARLY

A. 700   B. 725   C. 750   D. 775

13. In the sketch shown at the right, the angle X is
    A. 129°00'
    B. 129°15'
    C. 129°30'
    D. 129°45'

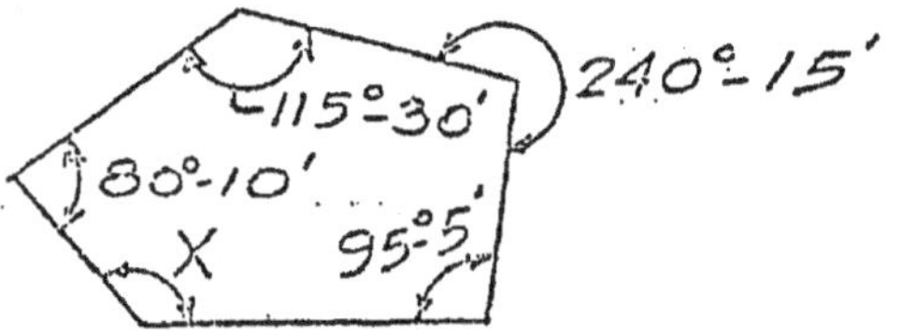

14. The number of board feet in eight pieces of 2" x 4" lumber, each of which is 12'6" long, is MOST NEARLY

A. 52   B. 59   C. 67   D. 73

15. The total number of cubic yards of concrete in twelve footings, each of which measures 6'6" x 9'3" x 18" is MOST NEARLY

A. 20   B. 40   C. 60   D. 80

16. If 7.5 gallons = 1 cu.ft., the total number of gallons of water in a tank 30 feet in diameter filled to a depth of 16'6" is MOST NEARLY

    A. 75,400   B. 87,500   C. 92,300   D. 98,600

17. The value of 600/5! is equal to

    A. 1500   B. 150   C. 50   D. 5

18. The trigonometric expression $1-\cos^2 x$ is equal to

    A. $\sin^2 x$ B. $\sin 1/2\ x$ C. $\sin 2x$ D. $\sin 1/x$

19. The value of is equal to MOST NEARLY

    A. 20.8   B. 21.1   C. 23.4   D. 25.7

20. In the equation $x^3 + x^2 + x - x^0 = y$, the value of y when x = 2 is

    A. 11   B. 12   C. 13   D. 14

21. Bituminous material is applied at a rate of 0.30 gallon per square yard over 1675 linear feet of a road 60 feet wide. The number of gallons of material used is MOST NEARLY

    A. 1675   B. 3350   C. 5025   D. 6700

22. The value of 0.6042' is, in inches, MOST NEARLY

    A. 7   B. 7 1/8   C. 7 1/4   D. 7 1/2

23.

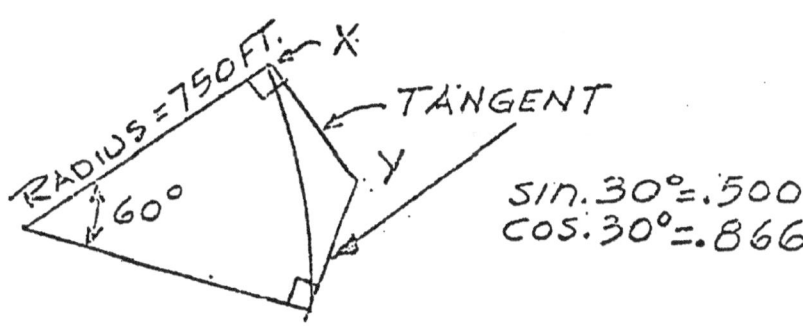

In the sketch shown above, the tangent XY is, in feet, MOST NEARLY

    A. 250   B. 322   C. 387   D. 433

24. In the cube drawn at the right, the diagonal XY is MOST NEARLY equal to
    A. 3.0
    B. 3.5
    C. 4.0
    D. 4.5

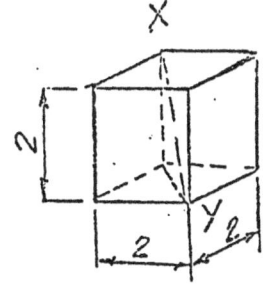

25. The readings on the horizontal plate of a transit for an angle measured three times by repetition is 220°45'12". The angle is MOST NEARLY

   A. 74°50'3"   B. 73°35'4"   C. 72°22'3"   D. 71°18'4"

KEY (CORRECT ANSWERS)

1. B
2. D
3. D
4. B
5. A

6. A
7. C
8. C
9. D
10. A

11. B
12. C
13. C
14. C
15. B

16. B
17. D
18. A
19. C
20. C

21. B
22. C
23. D
24. B
25. B

TEST 2

DIRECTIONS: Each question or incomplete statement is followed by several suggested answers or completions. Select the one that BEST answers the question or completes the statement. *PRINT THE LETTER OF THE CORRECT ANSWER IN THE SPACE AT THE RIGHT.*

1. The arithmetic mean of the values 0, 3, 4, 6, and 7 is 1.____
   A. 3 B. 4 C. 5 D. 6

2. The total number of 9" x 9" asphalt tiles needed to cover the area shown in the floor plan drawn at the right is MOST NEARLY 2.____
   A. 304
   B. 332
   C. 368
   D. 408

3. One radian is MOST NEARLY equal to 3.____
   A. 57° B. 58° C. 59° D. 60°

4. Cos 260° is equal to 4.____
   A. + cos 80° B. +sin 80° C. -sin 80° D. -cos 80°

5. The weight of twelve 8 WF 13 beams, 15'0" long, is, in pounds, MOST NEARLY 5.____
   A. 2100 B. 2350 C. 2500 D. 3100

6. Of the following chemicals, the one that would MOST likely be used to disinfect a potable water tank is 6.____
   A. fluorine B. bromine C. cadmium D. chlorine

7. The chemical symbol for tin is 7.____
   A. Ti B. Sn C. Ru D. Z

8. Of the following, the one that is MOST often used as an alloying element in stainless steel is 8.____
   A. tin B. silver C. aluminum D. chromium

9. Of the following materials used to make pipes, the one that is MOST resistant to the corrosive action of acids is 9.____
   A. vitrified clay B. concrete
   C. cast iron D. steel

10. The electrolyte in a car battery is _____ acid. 10.____
    A. sulfuric B. nitric C. hydrochloric D. picric

11. In the sketch of the open traverse shown at the right, the bearing of line MN is
    A. S63° W
    B. N37° W
    C. S43° E
    D. N65° W

Questions 12-13.

DIRECTIONS: In answering Questions 12 and 13, refer to the following notes on surveying leveling.

STA.	B.S.	H.I.	F.S.	ELEV.
BM1	6.72			87.50
TP1	8.52		4.63	
BM2			7.34	

12. The H.I. of TP1 is
    A. 96.25   B. 98.11   C. 100.43   D. 102.30

13. The ELEV. of BM2 is
    A. 90.77   B. 94.32   C. 96.75   D. 99.45

14. In the sketch shown at the right, the method used to locate point X is called the _____ method.
    A. scalar
    B. polar
    C. offset
    D. resection

15. The stadia method is MOST often used in _____ surveys.
    A. topographic   B. triangulation   C. photogrammetric   D. geodetic

16. The workability of freshly mixed concrete is measured
    A. with a Rockwell machine
    B. by the proctor method
    C. by a slump test
    D. with a Casagrande cup

17. To permit easy removal, the interior surfaces of concrete forms are usually coated with
    A. lacquer
    B. oil
    C. sal ammoniac
    D. lime water

18. Of the following, the one that is MOST likely to be measured with a micrometer caliper is the

    A. flange width of a beam
    B. gap of a spark plug
    C. thickness of sheet steel
    D. pitch of a gear

19. Reinforcing bars in mats are tied together by tie wire. Of the following, the BEST reason for this practice is to

    A. ground the mat
    B. decrease the bond stress in the bars
    C. hold the bars in place during pouring
    D. give the bars structural continuity in both directions

20. In a 1:2.5:3.75 concrete mix, the 3.75 represents the amount of

    A. water
    B. cement
    C. sand
    D. coarse aggregate

21. The method used in determining grain size distribution of sand is called _____ analysis.

    A. Atterberg limits
    B. sieve
    C. hydrometer
    D. CBR

22. Of the following materials, the one that is LEAST suitable as backfill material is one containing

    A. peat
    B. sand
    C. gravel
    D. crushed stone

23. The liquid that collects on the horizontal surface of freshly poured concrete is called

    A. efflorescence
    B. laitance
    C. slime
    D. mortar

24. Of the following, the MOST important requirement of a written inspection report is

    A. length
    B. neatness
    C. promptness
    D. accuracy

25. A *shake* is a defect found in

    A. glass   B. steel   C. timber   D. cast iron

KEY (CORRECT ANSWERS)

1. B
2. C
3. A
4. D
5. B

6. D
7. B
8. D
9. A
10. A

11. B
12. B
13. A
14. B
15. A

16. C
17. B
18. C
19. C
20. D

21. B
22. A
23. B
24. D
25. C

TEST 3

DIRECTIONS: Each question or incomplete statement is followed by several suggested answers or completions. Select the one that BEST answers the question or completes the statement. *PRINT THE LETTER OF THE CORRECT ANSWER IN THE SPACE AT THE RIGHT.*

1. A type of fire extinguisher that should NOT be used for a fire around electrical equipment is the _____ type. 1._____

    A. dry chemical
    B. carbon dioxide
    C. water solution
    D. liquified gas

2. Doors on the outside face of buildings frequently open outward. Of the following, the BEST reason for this is 2._____

    A. to save lobby space
    B. to allow easy exit from the building in an emergency
    C. they are less expensive when they open outward
    D. they are easier to hang when opening outward

3. Of the following, the one that is a safety device used is an electric circuit is a 3._____

    A. solenoid   B. capacitor   C. fuse   D. bus bar

4. 4._____

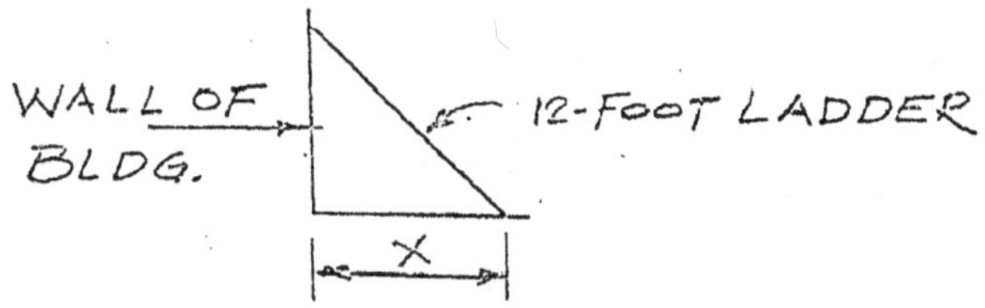

    When a 12-foot ladder is to be raised against the wall of a building as shown in the sketch above, safety requires that the distance from the wall to the base of the ladder, as represented by X, should be _____ ft.

    A. 1   B. 2   C. 3   D. 4

5. Of the following actions, the one which should NOT be taken in administering first aid to a person with a nosebleed is to 5._____

    A. make the person sit with his head tilted back
    B. keep the person in a lying position with head and shoulders raised
    C. pack the bleeding nostril lightly and then pinch the nose
    D. make the person walk about with his head tilted to the side

6. *Curb valves shall be NRS gate type designed for a minimum of 125 psi working pressure.*
    As used in the specification above, NRS means 6._____

    A. nickel rust-proof steel
    B. neutral, reverse, standard
    C. neutral, right, straight
    D. non-rising stem

7. *Chemical analyses and physical tests shall be made as provided in the ASTM specifications.*
   As used in the specification above, ASTM means

   A. Analytic System for Testing of Materials
   B. Automatic Scientific Testing of Materials
   C. American Society for Testing and Materials
   D. Association of Scientific Testers of Materials

8. Certain specifications call for Phillips head screws. Of the following drawings, the one that represents the Phillips head screw is

   A.   B.   C.   D.

9. *Galvanizing shall be in accordance with ASTM 153-42T.* As used in the specification above, galvanizing means coating with

   A. tin   B. nickel   C. titanium   D. zinc

10. Included in a hardware specification is a paragraph entitled *butts*. Butts are usually used on

    A. doors   B. windows   C. louvers   D. screens

11. *The work shall include all ornamental quoins, rowlock or soldier courses.*
    The statement above is from a specification for

    A. glazing
    C. carpentry
    B. brick work
    D. plumbing

12. *The exterior surfaces of the pump, the exposed surfaces of the bedplate and any other parts subject to rusting shall be sandblasted and given a minimum of three coats of paint, having a finished thickness of not less than 15 mils of Tarset Primer coal tar epoxy.*
    As used in the specifications above, 15 mils is, in inches, MOST NEARLY equal to

    A. 1/64   B. 1/32   C. 1/16   D. 3/32

13. *The term "rock excavation" shall mean rock, boulders or old concrete over one-half cubic yard in size which cannot be dislodged or removed without drilling. Compensation for "rock excavation" shall be made on the unit prices quoted or established in the Form of Proposal.* Compensation for *rock excavation* is MOST often paid as a unit price per

    A. ton of rock
    B. cubic yard *of* rock
    C. piece of rock over one-half cubic yard
    D. truck load of rock

14. *All reinforcement shall be bent cold. The minimum radius of bend shall be 4 diameters for a number 5 bar or smaller and 6 diameters for larger bars.*
    According to the above specification, the minimum radius of bend for a number 6 bar would be

    A. 3"   B. 3 1/2"   C. 4"   D. 4 1/2"

15. *Coupling for the Richmond Conduit shall be a 36-inch sleeve type Dresser Coupling, Style 38 with Grade 27 rubber gasket.*
    The dresser coupling specified above

    A. is a flanged coupling B. is a flexible coupling
    C. requires field welding D. is a boltless coupling

16. Of the following, the one that is NOT part of a window is a

    A. mullion B. muntin C. sill D. saddle

17. A vertical wood member in the wall of a wood frame house is known as a

    A. stringer B. ridge member
    C. stud D. rafter

18. A cast iron bell and spigot elbow fitting having a bend of 22 1/2 degrees is commonly called a _____ bend.

    A. 1/16 B. 1/8 C. 1/4 D. 1/2

19. A purlin would be used

    A. on the side of a building
    B. on the roof of a building
    C. in the foundation of a building
    D. nowhere on building construction

20. In the elevation drawn at the right, the flange labeled X is known as a(n) _____ flange.
    A. expansion
    B. plug
    C. back
    D. blind

21. Of the following species of woods, the one that is classified as a soft wood is

    A. hickory B. ash C. walnut D. cedar

22. The continuation of an exterior wall above the roof line of a building is called a

    A. kiosk B. bulkhead C. shell D. parapet

23. Of the following pieces of construction equipment, the one MOST often used to excavate a trench in order to lay a water line from the water main in the street to a house is a

    A. bulldozer B. backhoe
    C. orange-peel bucket D. drag line

24. A humidity-sensing element is called a(n)

    A. aquastat B. thermostat
    C. hygrostat D. rheostat

25. The ends of wood posts that are to be set in the ground are MOST often coated with   25.____
    A. red lead   B. creosote   C. varnish   D. shellac

KEY (CORRECT ANSWERS)

1. C
2. B
3. C
4. C
5. D

6. D
7. C
8. A
9. D
10. A

11. B
12. A
13. B
14. D
15. B

16. D
17. C
18. A
19. B
20. D

21. D
22. D
23. B
24. C
25. B

TEST 4

DIRECTIONS: Each question or incomplete statement is followed by several suggested answers or completions. Select the one that BEST answers the question or completes the statement. *PRINT THE LETTER OF THE CORRECT ANSWER IN THE SPACE AT THE RIGHT.*

1.

   [Sketch: BAR X, 3/4" EXPANSION JOINT (SEALED), CONCR. PAVEMENT — ELEVATION]

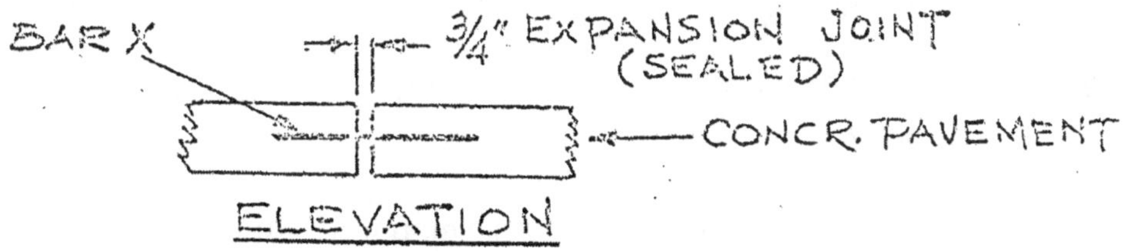

   In the elevation sketched above, the Bar X is known as a

   A. shim   B. spline   C. kerf   D. dowel

   1.____

2. The invert of sewer pipe is the _____ of the pipe.

   A. inside of the crown
   B. outside of the crown
   C. inside of the bottom
   D. outside of the bottom

   2.____

3. A batter pile is one that is

   A. damaged
   B. driven at an angle
   C. made of prestressed concrete
   D. made of hollow shell steel

   3.____

4. A stairway with 7 treads usually has _____ risers.

   A. 6   B. 7   C. 8   D. 9

   4.____

5. The practice of keeping a freshly poured concrete walkway moist for a minimum period of seven days is called

   A. buffing
   B. curing
   C. tempering
   D. puddling

   5.____

6. A tie rod is designed primarily to carry _____ stresses.

   A. torsional
   B. tension
   C. shear
   D. bearing

   6.____

7. The type of valve used to allow the flow of water only in one direction is a _____ valve.

   A. check
   B. butterfly
   C. double disk gate
   D. balanced

   7.____

8. The reinforcing bar shape shown at the right usually found in a concrete

   A. slab
   B. column
   C. wall
   D. beam

   8.____

9. The type of pipe in which the joints are caulked with lead is _____ pipe.
   A. copper   B. steel   C. cast iron   D. brass

10. The method LEAST likely to be used in fastening steel structural members together is
    A. riveting   B. bolting   C. brazing   D. welding

11. A scale of 1/240 is the same as a scale of _____ inch equals _____ foot(feet).
    A. 1/4; 1   B. 3/4; 1   C. 1; 20   D. 1; 24

12. The symbol ⁓⁓⁓⁓ on a topographic map represents a
    A. party wall   B. match line
    C. hedge   D. fence line

13. The plan drawn above represents a window in a _____ wall.
    A. brick   B. reinforced concrete
    C. wood frame   D. brick veneer

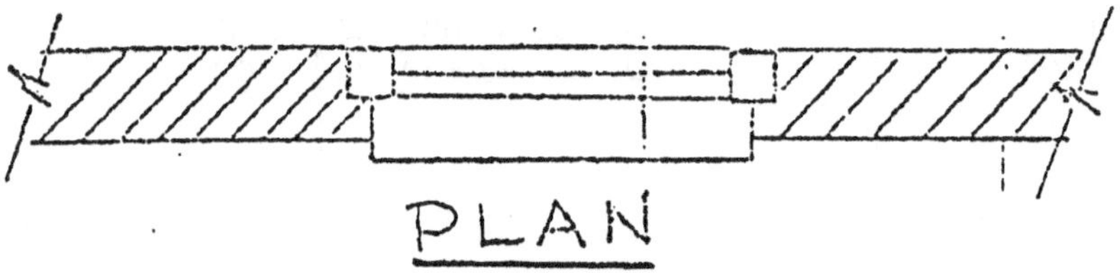

14. In the elevation shown at the right, the flared hole is known as a _____ hole.
    A. tapered
    B. countersunk
    C. spotfaced
    D. counterbored

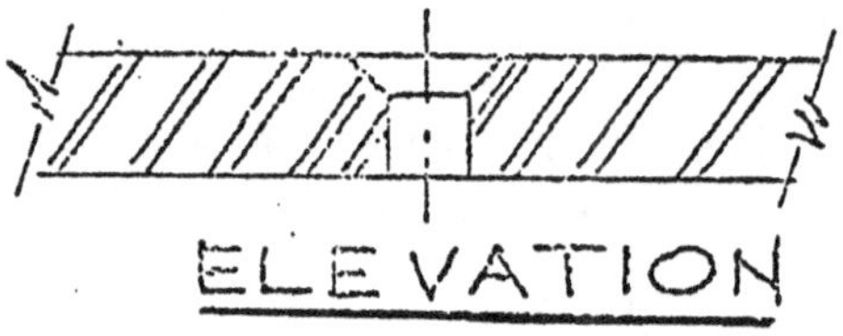

15. 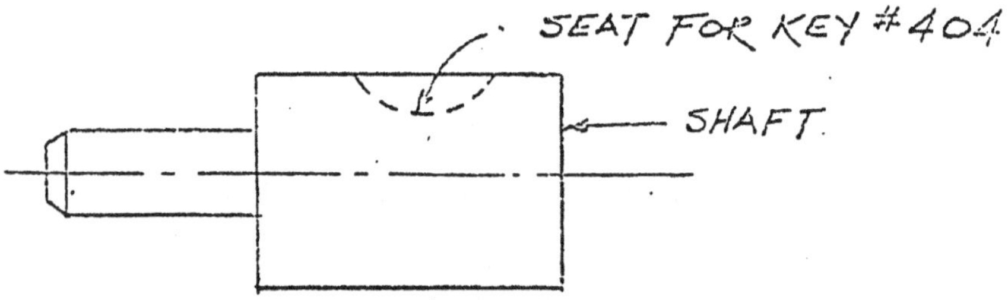 In the sketch of a shaft shown above, the type of key referred to is a _____ key.
    A. Barth   B. Kennedy   C. Lewis   D. Woodruff

16. The weld symbol shown at the right indicates a _____ weld.
    A. bead
    B. groove
    C. plug
    D. fillet

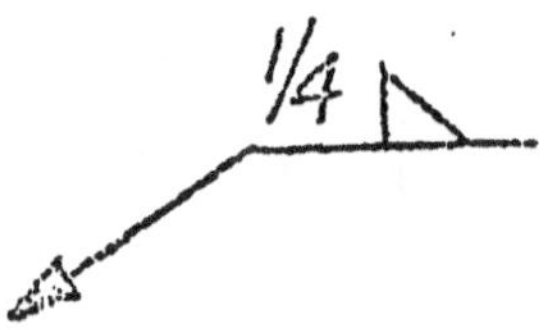

17. A beam compass is particularly useful for

    A. detailing reinforcing bars
    B. drawing circular arcs of large radius
    C. computing areas from scale drawings
    D. structural detailing

18. The symbol —⋈— appearing on a diagrammatic piping drawing represents a _____ valve.

    A. globe
    B. three-way
    C. angle
    D. butterfly

19. The symbol shown at the right represents a _____ tee.
    A. screwed
    B. flanged
    C. bell and spigot
    D. welded

20. The notation N.T.S. appearing on an engineering drawing means

    A. not to scale
    B. not to be sanded
    C. notch top surface
    D. not too steep

21. In inking tracings, which of the following will tend to *increase* the thickness of an inked line?

    A. A small amount of ink in the pen
    B. Rapid movement of the pen on the paper
    C. Leaning the pen more to the paper
    D. A hard working surface

22. Of the following instruments, the one that is used in a drafting office to estimate the area of tracts of land shown on a topographic map is a

    A. planimeter
    B. clinometer
    C. pantograph
    D. geodimeter

23. The sketch shown at the right represents the front view or elevation of a solid object. Of the following, the one that CANNOT correctly represent the left-side view is

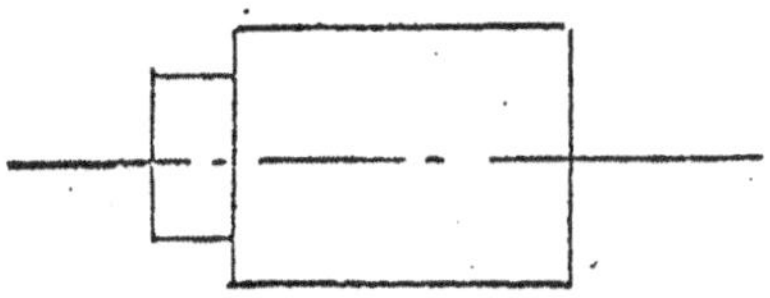

    A. 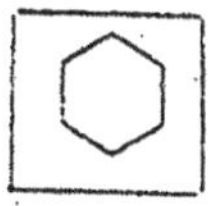 (hexagon in square)
    B.  (triangle in circle)
    C. 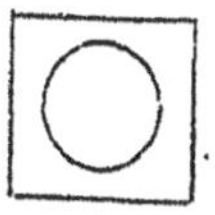 (circle in square)
    D. 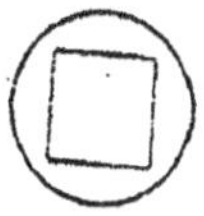 (square in circle)

24.

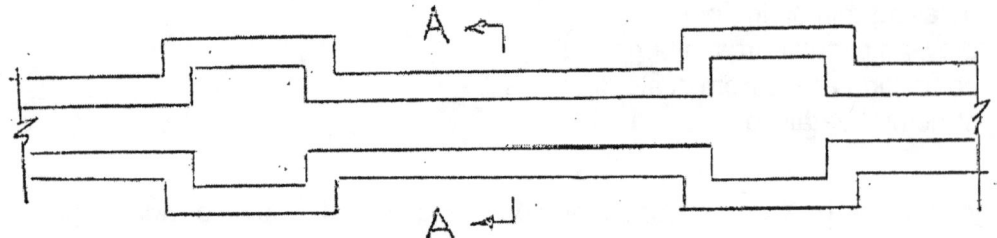

Part of a foundation plan appears as shown above. Section A-A would appear MOST likely as in

A.    B. 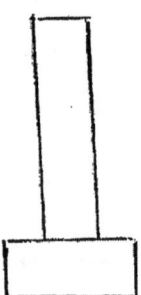   C.    D.

25. The sketch shown at the right shows a plan of an object. Section F-F should be shown as in

A.

B.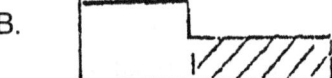

C.

D.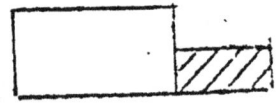

KEY (CORRECT ANSWERS)

1. D
2. C
3. B
4. C
5. B

6. B
7. A
8. D
9. C
10. C

11. C
12. C
13. A
14. B
15. D

16. D
17. B
18. A
19. B
20. A

21. C
22. A
23. A
24. B
25. C

EXAMINATION SECTION
TEST 1

DIRECTIONS: Each question or incomplete statement is followed by several suggested answers or completions. Select the one that BEST answers the question or completes the statement. *PRINT THE LETTER OF THE CORRECT ANSWER IN THE SPACE AT THE RIGHT.*

1. The elevation of Point A is 62.54 feet, and the elevation of Point B is 58.25 feet. The difference in elevation between points A and B is, in feet and inches, MOST NEARLY

    A. 4' 2 1/2"   B. 4' 3"   C. 4' 3 1/2"   D. 4' 4"

2. A line drawn from the midpoint of the hypotenuse of a right angle triangle to the opposite 90 degree angle is equal to

    A. the square root of the product of the two sides
    B. the average of the three sides
    C. the average of the two adjacent sides
    D. half the hypotenuse

3. The sum of all numbers from 1 to 30, inclusive, can be expressed as

    A. $\frac{1+31}{2} \times 30$ B. $\frac{1+31}{2} \times 29$ C. $\frac{1+31}{2} \times 30$ D. $\frac{1+29}{2} \times 30$

4. If the $\log_{10} 2 = 0.3010$, then the $\log_{10} 0.2$ is equal to

    A. 9.6990 - 10
    B. 9.3010 - 10
    C. -1.6990
    D. +.6990

5. The area of an equilateral triangle whose side is a, is

    A. $\frac{a^2}{2}$ B. $\frac{a^2 \sqrt{3}}{2}$ C. $3a^2 \sqrt{3}$ D. $\frac{a^2}{4} \sqrt{3}$

6. The square root of the sum of the squares of the numbers 5, 6, 7, and 8 is MOST NEARLY

    A. 16.5   B. 11.6   C. 9.8   D. 13.2

7. The surface area of a cube is equal to its volume. The length of a side is MOST NEARLY

    A. 2   B. 4   C. 6   D. 8

8. If $\frac{1}{F} = \frac{1}{f_1} + \frac{1}{f_2}$, then F is equal to

A. $f_1 + f_2$

B. $\dfrac{1}{f_1 + f_2}$

C. $\dfrac{f_1 f_2}{f_1 + f_2}$

D. $\dfrac{(f_1 + f_2)f_1}{f_2(f_1 - f_2)}$

9. If there are 640 acres in a square mile, the number of square feet in an acre is MOST NEARLY

   A. 41,320 B. 42,240 C. 42,980 D. 43,560

10. The formula for the quantity of water flowing over a weir is $Q = 3.33bh^{3/2}$. The rate of discharge of water, Q, when b = 5 and h = 2.5 is MOST NEARLY

    A. 50 B. 55 C. 60 D. 65

11. In the right angle triangle shown at the right, the length of line EF is equal to

    A. tan x + tan y
    B. tan x - tan y / 1 + tan x tan y
    C. tan (x+y)
    D. tan x + tan y / 1 - tan x tan y

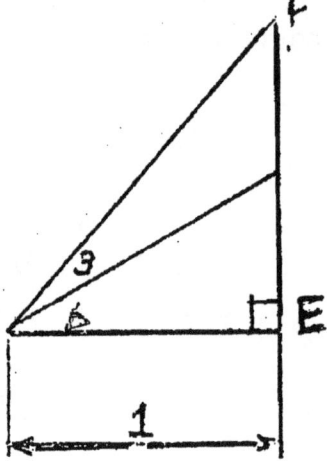

12. The volume of a solid is $h/6(b_1 + b_2 + 4m)$, where h is the height of the solid, b_1 is the area of one base, b_2 the area of the other base, and m the area halfway between the bases. The volume of the solid shown at the right is MOST NEARLY

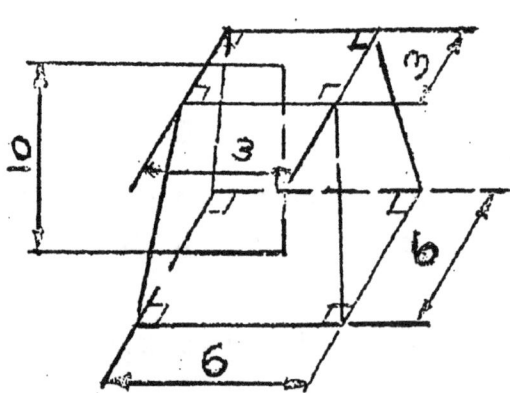

   A. 225
   B. 210
   C. 195
   D. 180

13.

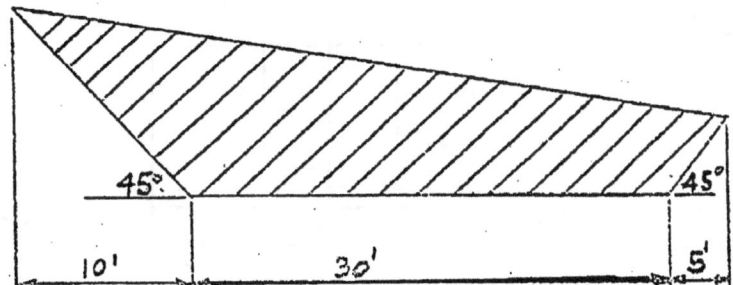

The cross-section area of the earth section shown above is, in square feet, MOST NEARLY

A. 300 B. 285 C. 280 D. 275

14. In the equation y = cos 3x, the value of y for x = 80° is MOST NEARLY

A. $+\dfrac{1}{2}$ B. $-\dfrac{1}{2}$ C. $\dfrac{\sqrt{3}}{2}$ D. $-\dfrac{\sqrt{3}}{2}$

15. The acceleration of a falling body is 32 feet per second. This means MOST NEARLY that the

A. distance the body falls is directly proportional to the time of fall
B. body falls with a uniform velocity
C. velocity of the body varies directly with time
D. velocity of the falling body varies as the square of the time of fall

16.

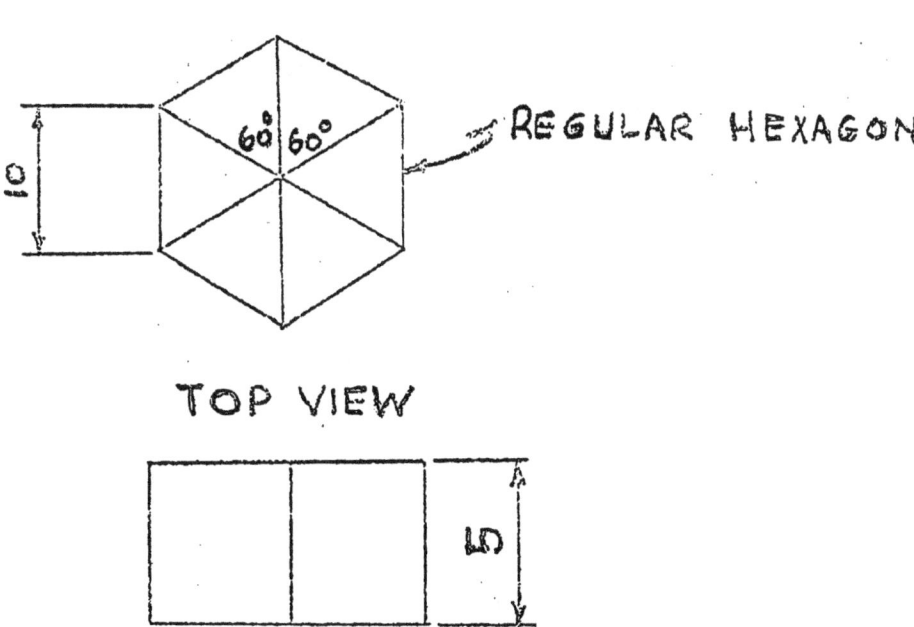

The volume of the solid shown above is MOST NEARLY

A. $275\sqrt{3}$ B. $275\sqrt{2}$ C. 350 D. $750\sqrt{3}$

17. The volume of the solid shown at the right is MOST NEARLY
    A. 336
    B. 294
    C. 272
    D. 259

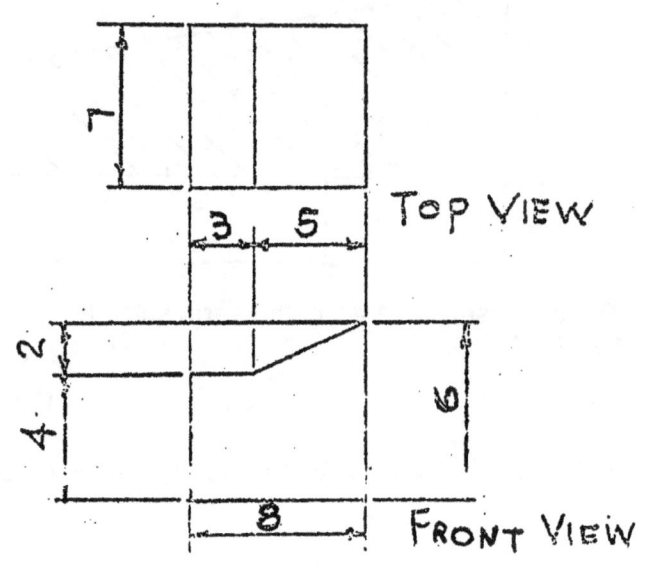

17____

18. A hole is cut from a plate as shown at the right. The area removed is, in square inches, MOST NEARLY
    A. 3.8
    B. 5.6
    C. 7.8
    D. 9.1

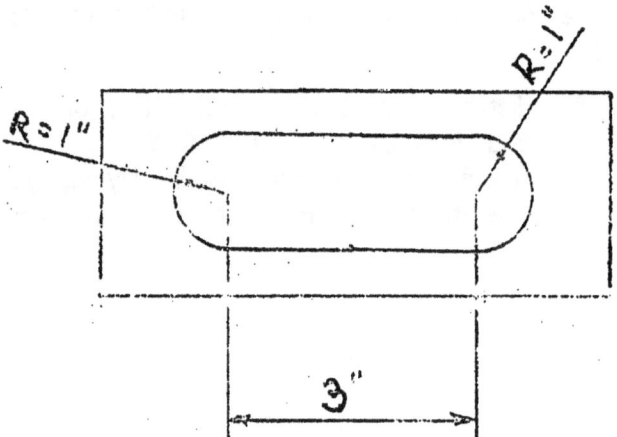

18____

19.

The cross-section area of the road slab shown on the previous page is, in square feet, MOST NEARLY

 A. 8.75   B. 8.87   C. 9.00   D. 9.12

20. The material for the slab in the above question is MOST likely

 A. asphalt   B. concrete
 C. Belgian block   D. gravel

21. The volume of the solid shown at the right is

 A. b^2h
 B. $b^2h \sec 60°$
 C. $b^2h \sin 60°$
 D. $b^2h \cos 60°$

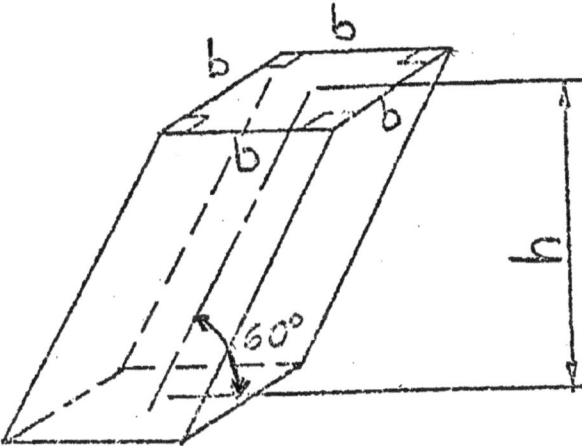

22.

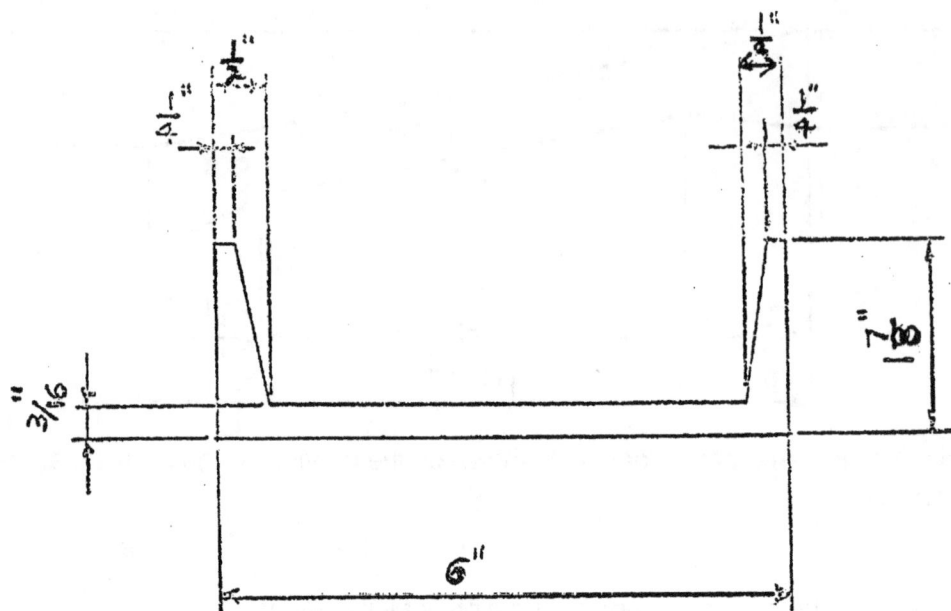

The cross-sectional area of the steel channel whose dimensions are as shown above is, in square inches, MOST NEARLY

A. 2.0   B. 2.2   C. 2.4   D. 2.6

23.

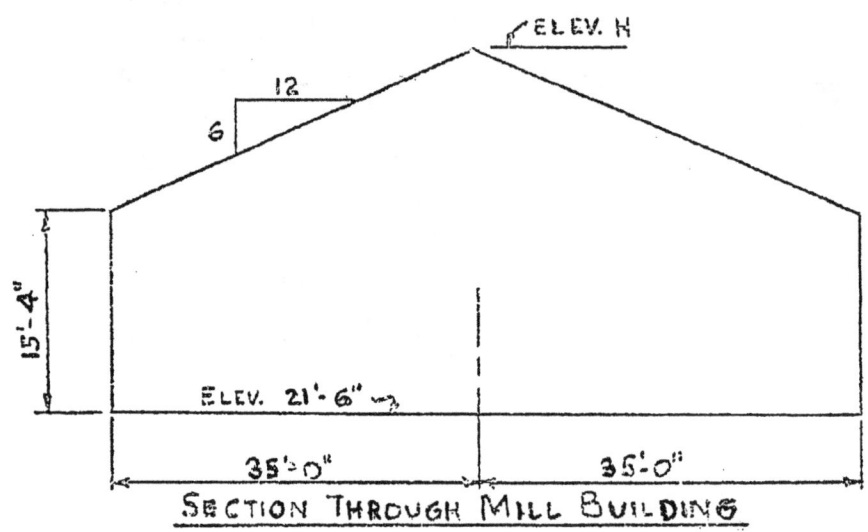

In the section shown above, the value of elevation H is, in feet and inches, MOST NEARLY

A. 71' 10"   B. 36' 10"   C. 39' 0"   D. 54' 4"

24. If the plotted curve for the equation y = sin x is as shown at the right, then the curve for the equation y = (sin x)² is MOST NEARLY as in

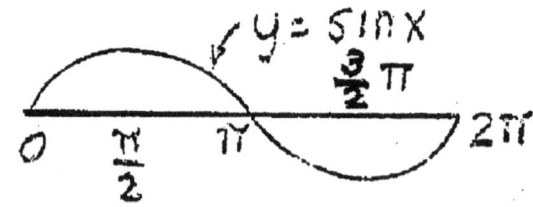

A.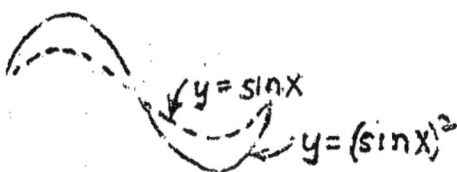

B.

C.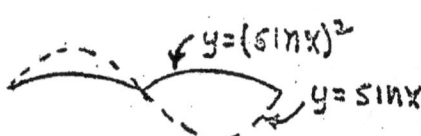

D.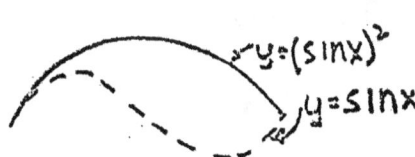

25. The ratio of the area of the 10' strip to the area of the entire plot is MOST NEARLY
    A. 0.33
    B. 0.28
    C. 0.23
    D. 0.18

25___

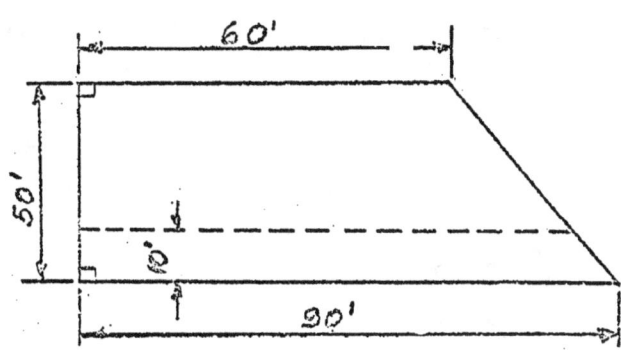

Questions 26-30.

DIRECTIONS: In Questions 26 through 30, inclusive, the top view and the front elevation of an object are shown at the left. At the right are four drawings, one of which represents the end elevation of the object as seen from the right. Select the drawing which represents the correct end elevation and print the letter of this drawing in the space at the right. The first group is shown as an example only. The CORRECT answer is C.

SAMPLE QUESTION

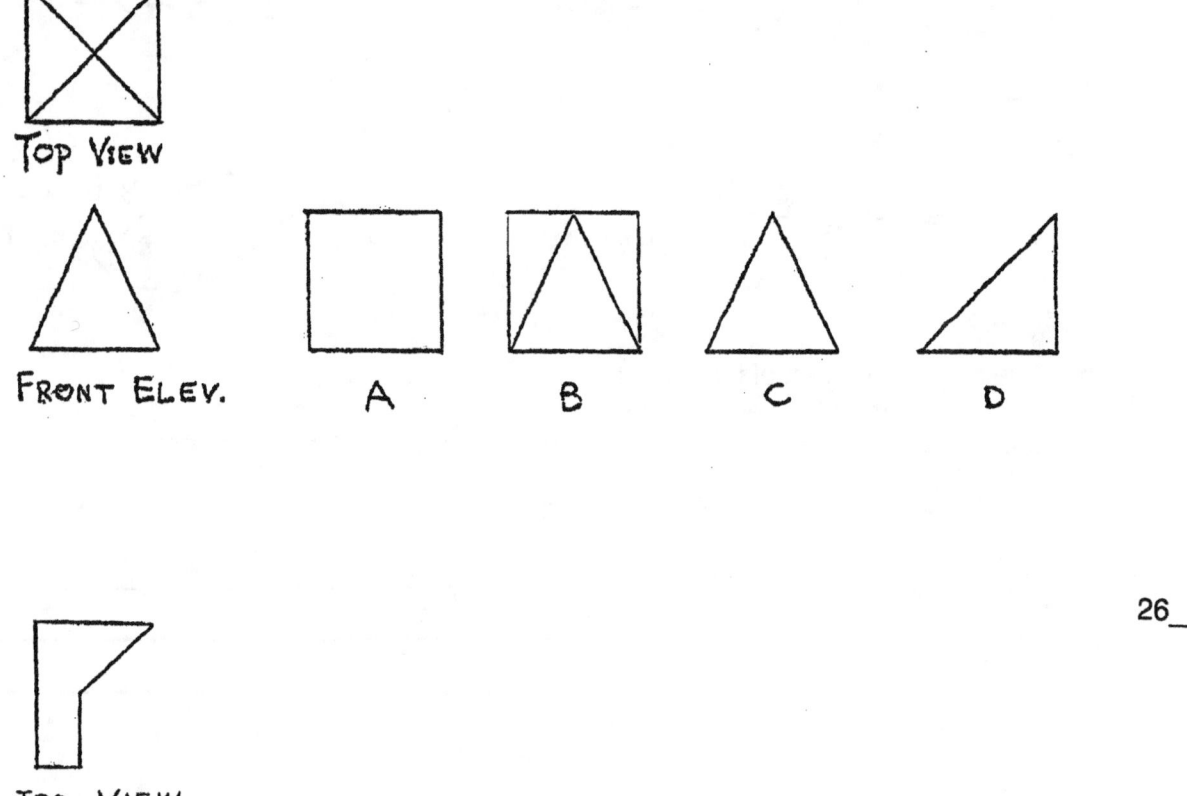

26.

27.

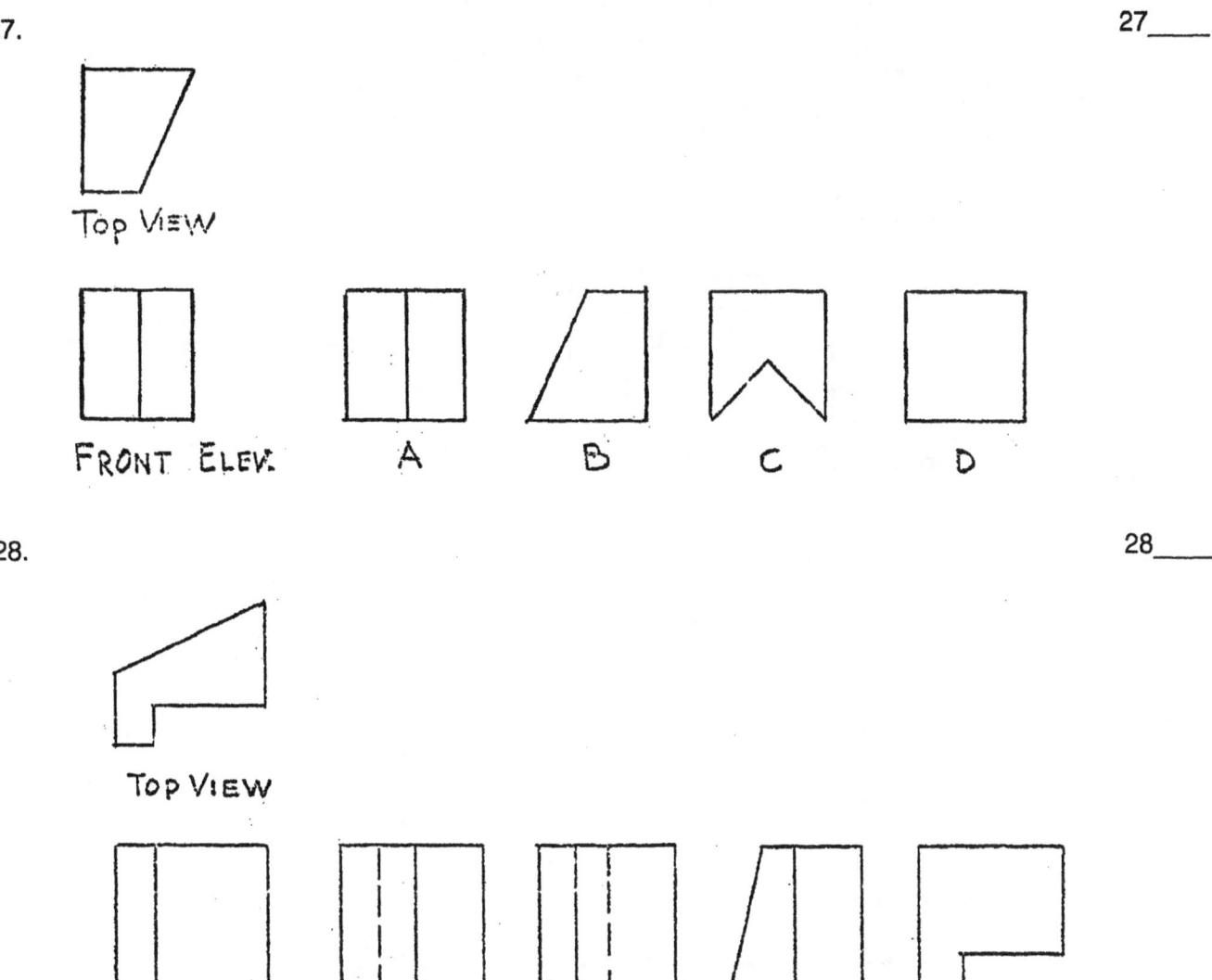

29.

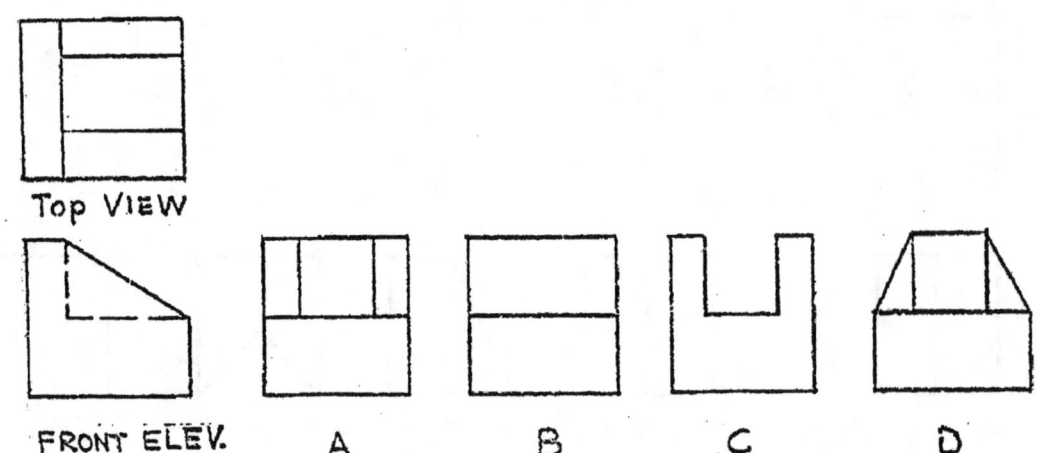

30.

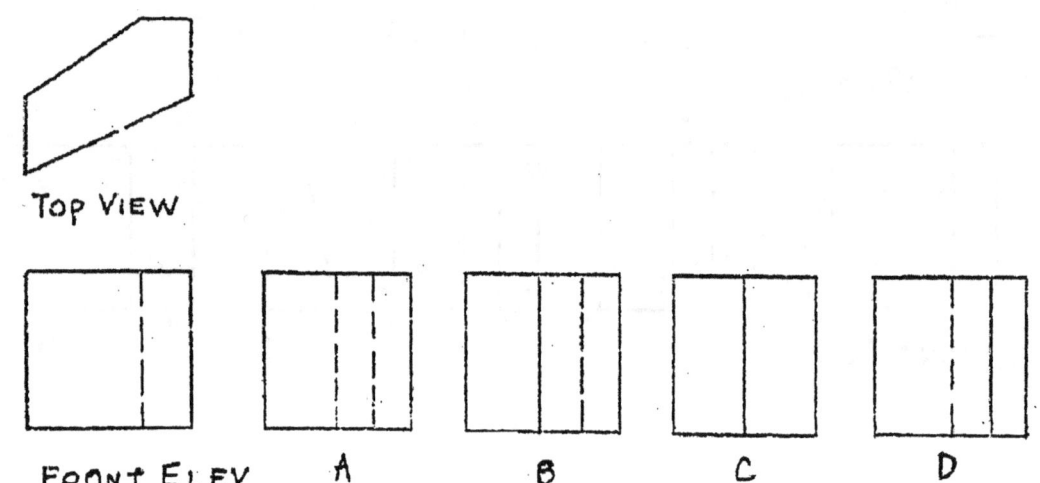

KEY (CORRECT ANSWERS)

1.	C	16.	D
2.	D	17.	D
3.	C	18.	D
4.	B	19.	A
5.	D	20.	B
6.	D	21.	A
7.	C	22.	C
8.	C	23.	D
9.	D	24.	C
10.	D	25.	C
11.	C	26.	C
12.	B	27.	D
13.	D	28.	B
14.	B	29.	A
15.	C	30.	C

TEST 2

DIRECTIONS: Each question or incomplete statement is followed by several suggested answers or completions. Select the one that BEST answers the question or completes the statement. *PRINT THE LETTER OF THE CORRECT ANSWER IN THE SPACE AT THE RIGHT.*

1. The same units apply to

    A. work and power
    B. power and energy
    C. work and energy
    D. force and power

    1____

2. Of the following, the one that contains but a single element is

    A. ozone
    B. carbohydrate
    C. hormone
    D. protein

    2____

3. Sodium is usually stored under kerosene or gasoline because

    A. it does not react with gasoline or kerosene
    B. it is soluble in gasoline or kerosene
    C. hydrocarbons purify sodium
    D. its presence in gasoline or kerosene prevents spontaneous combustion

    3____

4. The smallest particle of a compound that still contains the characteristic of the compound is a(n)

    A. electron
    B. proton
    C. atom
    D. molecule

    4____

5. Specifications state that a brick wall is to be washed with a weak solution of muriatic acid. The formula for muriatic acid is

    A. HFL
    B. HNO_3
    C. HCl
    D. H_2SO_4

    5____

6. The atomic number of an element is equal to the number of

    A. protons in the nucleus of the element
    B. electrons outside the nucleus
    C. electrons inside the nucleus
    D. protons outside the nucleus

    6____

7. The elements fluorine, chlorine, bromine, and iodine have the following characteristic in common:
   They have the same

    A. atomic number
    B. atomic weight
    C. number of electrons in the nucleus
    D. number of electrons in the outer ring

    7____

8. Of the following chemicals, the one that is LEAST active chemically is

    A. iron
    B. mercury
    C. zinc
    D. aluminum

    8____

9. SiO_2 is the chemical formula for

    A. limestone
    B. granite
    C. clay
    D. sand

    9____

10. The specific gravity of a liquid is 0.5. This means MOST NEARLY that the

  A. density of the liquid is 0.5
  B. mass of the liquid is 0.5g
  C. liquid is heavier than water
  D. weight of the liquid is approximately 31 pounds per cubic foot

11. The weight of a 2 cubic block is 300 pounds. The weight of this block when submerged in water, as shown at the right, would be, in pounds, MOST NEARLY
  A. 424
  B. 362
  C. 238
  D. 175

12. An automobile moving 30 miles per hour is moving MOST NEARLY _____ feet per second.

  A. 30 B. 35 C. 40 D. 45

13. The hydraulic radius of a sewer for a given depth of flow is equal to the cross-sectional area in square feet of that part of the sewer filled with water divided by the surface of the sewer in feet in contact with water.
The hydraulic radius of a 4-foot diameter sewer flowing half full is, in feet, MOST NEARLY

  A. 1 B. 2 C. 4 D. 8

14.

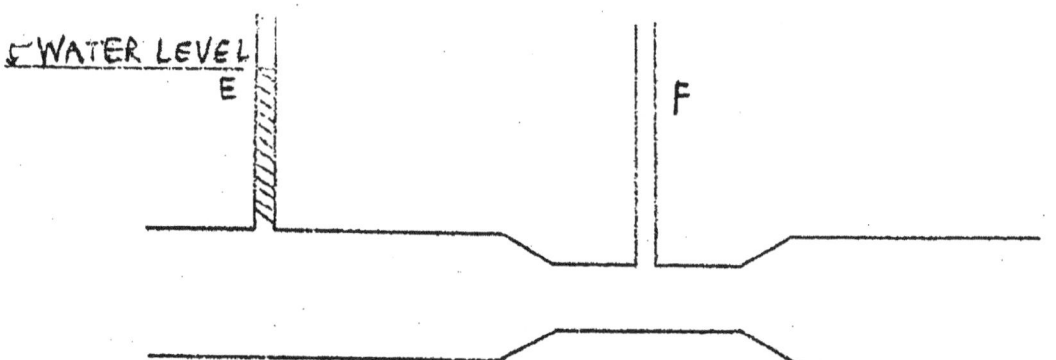

Water is flowing through the pipe with a reducing unit as shown above. The level of the water in gage F will be

  A. lower than in gage E

B. higher than in gage E
C. at the same level as in gage E
D. at a higher or lower level than in gage E, depending upon the flow

15. The force F needed to hold the system in equilibrium is, in pounds, MOST NEARLY
    A. 50
    B. 86.7
    C. 100
    D. 141

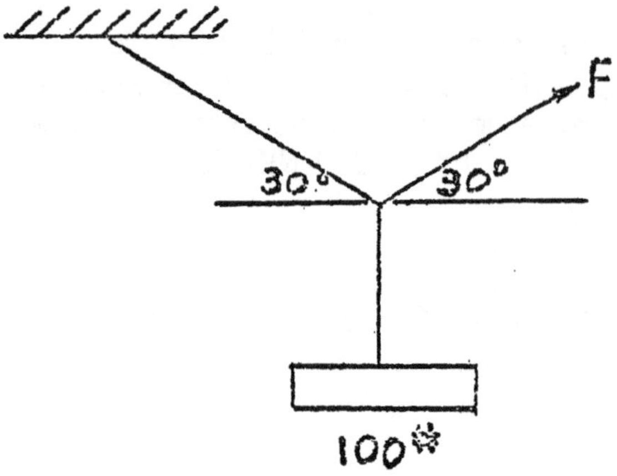

16. Of the following states of water, the one having the greatest heat content is usually

    A. water at 32°F
    B. ice at 32°F
    C. water at 212°F
    D. steam at 212°F

17. A window jamb usually refers to the _____ the window.

    A. method of securing
    B. frame immediately above
    C. frame immediately below
    D. frame adjacent to the side of

18. An object is traveling at 60 miles per hour. Its speed, in feet per second, is MOST NEARLY

    A. 30   B. 44   C. 88   D. 96

19. A force of one pound acting on a body weighing one pound will produce (neglect friction) a(n) _____ per second.

    A. velocity of 1 foot
    B. acceleration of 1 foot per second
    C. velocity of 32 feet
    D. acceleration of 32 feet per second

Questions 20-24.

DIRECTIONS: Questions 20 through 24, inclusive, refer to the diagram shown below.

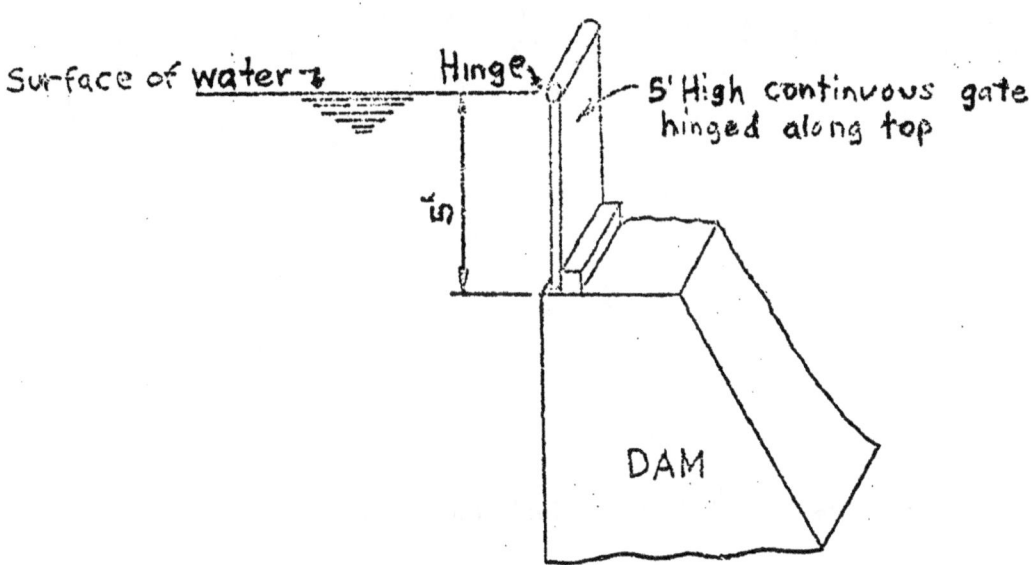

20. The unit pressure, in pounds per square foot, five (5) feet below the surface is MOST NEARLY

    A. 62.4   B. 2.3   C. 1560   D. 312

21. The unit pressure, in pounds per square inch, five (5) feet below the surface is MOST NEARLY

    A. 2.17   B. .85   C. .434   D. 2.30

22. The total force on a one-foot longitudinal section of the 5' gate is, in pounds, MOST NEARLY

    A. 585   B. 390   C. 780   D. 1560

23. The center of gravity of the forces acting on the gate is, in feet below the surface, MOST NEARLY

    A. 2.5   B. 3.0   C. 3.33   D. 3.67

24. The turning moment acting on a one-foot length of gate caused by the water is, in pound feet, MOST NEARLY

    A. 1200   B. 1600   C. 2000   D. 2600

25. The reaction R_L is

A. Wa/c+d B. Wb/c+d
C. We/c+d D. Wd/c+d

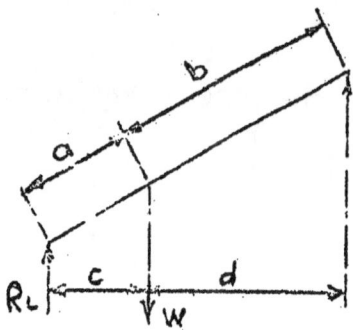

Questions 26-27.

DIRECTIONS: Questions 26 and 27 refer to the following diagram.

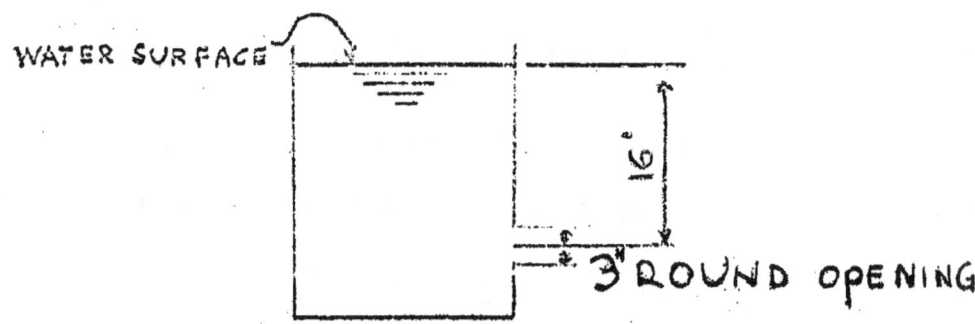

26. The velocity of the water leaving the 3" orifice is, in feet per second, MOST NEARLY 26____

    A. 8   B. 16   C. 32   D. 64

27. In the above diagram, if the water issues from the orifice horizontally with a velocity of 15 feet per second the distance E it will travel horizontally in 2 seconds is, in feet, MOST NEARLY 27____

    A. 15   B. 22.5   C. 30   D. 37.5

Questions 28-29.

DIRECTIONS: Questions 28 and 29 refer to the diagram shown below.

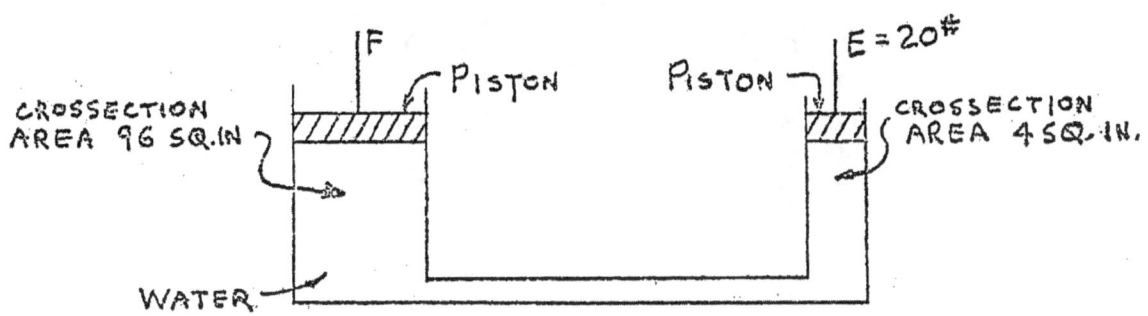

28. The gage pressure in the system shown above is, in pounds per square inch, MOST NEARLY

    A. 5　　B. 20　　C. 384　　D. 96

29. If the force applied at E were to move downward a distance of 12 inches, the load at F would move _____ inch(es).

    A. upward 12
    B. upward 4
    C. upward 1/2
    D. downward 12

30. If the 40# load is resting on the inclined plane and the coefficient of friction between plane and load is 0.6, then the #40 load
    A. will remain at rest
    B. will accelerate at a velocity of 3 feet per second per second
    C. will accelerate with a velocity of 4 feet per second per second
    D. will move down the incline with a uniform velocity

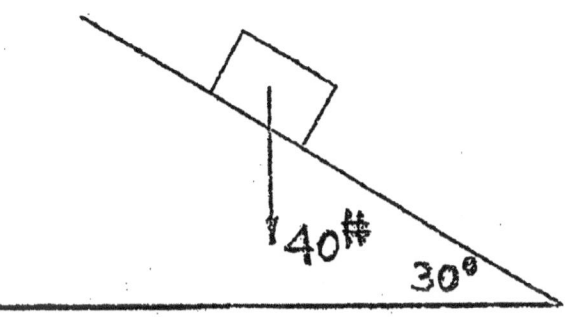

KEY (CORRECT ANSWERS)

1. C
2. A
3. A
4. D
5. C

6. A / B
7. D
8. B
9. D
10. D

11. D
12. D
13. A
14. A
15. C

16. D
17. D
18. C
19. D
20. D

21. A
22. C
23. C
24. D
25. D

26. C
27. C
28. A
29. C
30. A

TEST 3

DIRECTIONS: Each question or incomplete statement is followed by several suggested answers or completions. Select the one that BEST answers the question or completes the statement. *PRINT THE LETTER OF THE CORRECT ANSWER IN THE SPACE AT THE RIGHT.*

1.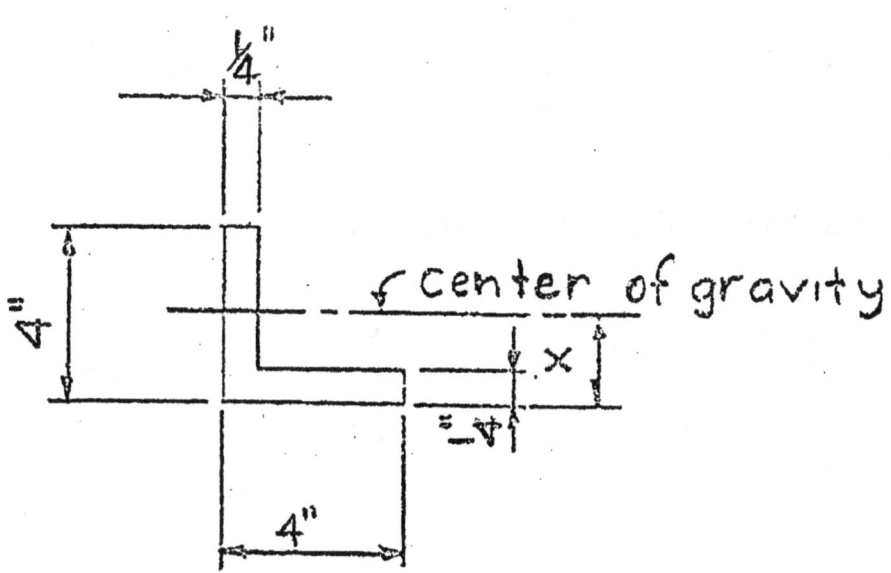

    In the 4" x 4" x 1/4" angle shown above, the distance X from the center of gravity of the angle to the base of the angle is, in inches, MOST NEARLY

    A. .9   B. 1.0   C. 1.1   D. 1.2

2. Torque is an action MOST NEARLY similar to

    A. compressing   B. shearing
    C. twisting   D. bending

3. The primary ingredient in wall plaster is

    A. gypsum   B. clay   C. sand   D. cement

Questions 4-6.

DIRECTIONS: Questions 4 through 6, inclusive, are to be answered on the basis of the sketch on the following page.

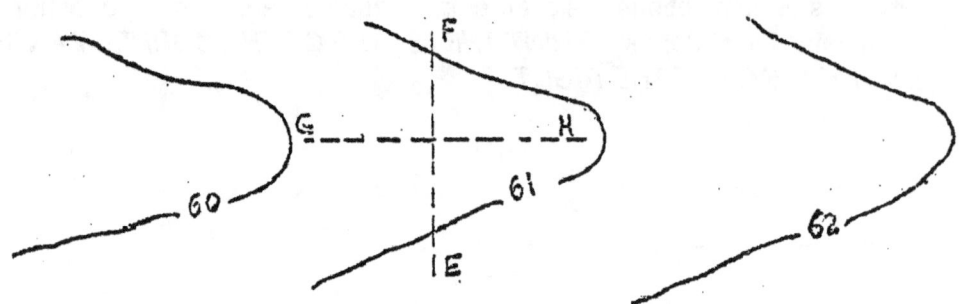

4. A surveyor, measuring from E to F, finds the terrain MOST NEARLY as in   4____

A.    B.

C.    D.

5. A surveyor, in measuring from G to H, finds the terrain MOST NEARLY as in   5____

A. ————————   B.

C.    D. ⌣

6. If the horizontal distance between successive contour lines is 100 feet, the slope of the ground is, in percent, MOST NEARLY   6____

    A. 2   B. 1   C. 1/2   D. 1/4

7. Reinforcing steel is to be placed for a concrete canopy. The steel would MOST likely be placed as in   7____

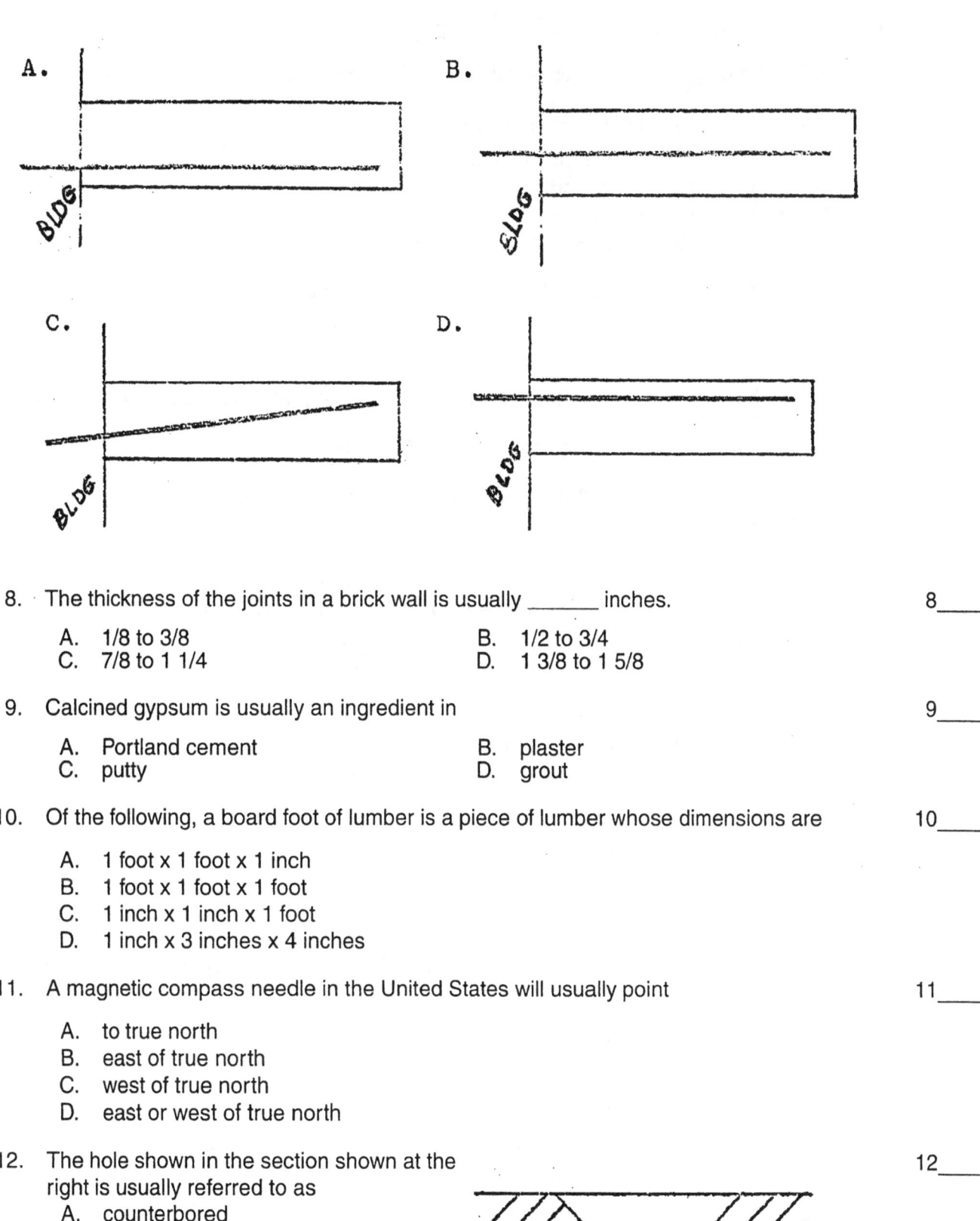

8. The thickness of the joints in a brick wall is usually _____ inches.

   A. 1/8 to 3/8
   B. 1/2 to 3/4
   C. 7/8 to 1 1/4
   D. 1 3/8 to 1 5/8

9. Calcined gypsum is usually an ingredient in

   A. Portland cement
   B. plaster
   C. putty
   D. grout

10. Of the following, a board foot of lumber is a piece of lumber whose dimensions are

    A. 1 foot x 1 foot x 1 inch
    B. 1 foot x 1 foot x 1 foot
    C. 1 inch x 1 inch x 1 foot
    D. 1 inch x 3 inches x 4 inches

11. A magnetic compass needle in the United States will usually point

    A. to true north
    B. east of true north
    C. west of true north
    D. east or west of true north

12. The hole shown in the section shown at the right is usually referred to as
    A. counterbored
    B. countersunk
    C. recessed
    D. reamed

13. An ordinary micrometer caliper will read directly to

    A. .01 inch B. .001 inch C. .00001 inch D. .01 foot

14. A flywheel on an engine is used primarily to

    A. store and release energy of rotation
    B. minimize foundation vibration
    C. reduce torsional vibration
    D. balance the shaft on which the flywheel is mounted

15. The machining operation of cutting a thread inside a drilled hole is known as

    A. reaming B. broaching C. boring D. tapping

16. The symbol ⎯⎯⏗⎯⎯ on the elevation of a plumbing drawing usually symbolizes a

    A. vent B. syphon C. trap D. drain

17. The current which a 60-watt bulb will draw in a 120-volt system is MOST NEARLY _____ ampere(s).

    A. 2 B. 1/4 C. 1/2 D. 4

18. Of the following units, the one which is NOT related to the field of illumination is the

    A. lumen   B. foot-candle
    C. candle-power   D. mho

19. Electricity is sometimes compared to the flow of water. Pressure of water is equivalent to which of the following terms in electricity?

    A. Current   B. Voltage
    C. Resistance   D. Conductivity

20. When two resistances each having a value R are connected in parallel, the total resistance is equal to

    A. R/4 B. R/2 C. 2R D. R

21. A transformer has 800 turns in the primary and 80 turns in the secondary. If the primary is connected to a 2200-volt line, the secondary voltage is MOST NEARLY

    A. 1100 B. 110 C. 220 D. 440

22. If an equal current is sent through the wires of the same length and material, but one has a larger diameter than the other,

    A. more heat will be produced in the larger wire
    B. more heat will be produced in the smaller wire
    C. a larger voltage drop will be produced in the larger wire
    D. less power will be dissipated in the smaller wire

23. A wire has an area of 100 circular mils. This means MOST NEARLY that the

    A. weight of the wire is .01 pound per foot
    B. area of the wire is .01 square inches

C. diameter of the wire is .01 inches
D. circumference of the wire is .01 inches

24.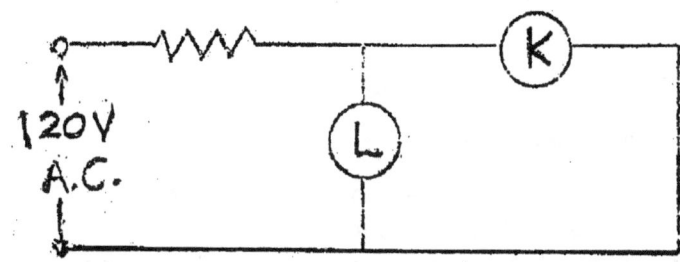

In the circuit shown above, the instrument marked K is a

A. voltmeter
B. frequency meter
C. wattmeter
D. ammeter

25.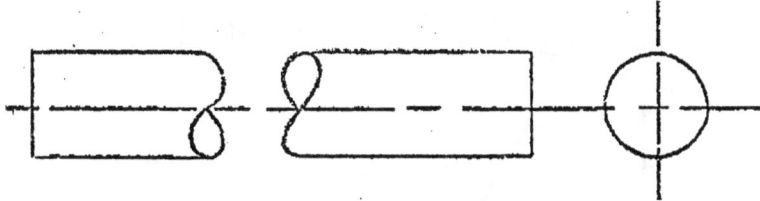

A rod may be shown on a drawing as above.
Of the following, the BEST reason for showing the break in the rod is that it

A. requires less space on the drawing
B. shows the type of material
C. lends an artistic touch to the drawing
D. shows the true shape of the cross-section

26. A note pointing to a hole on a plan view of a mechanical part is: *17/32 DRILL SPOT-FACE 15/16 DIA.* A section through this hole should look as in

A.
B.
C.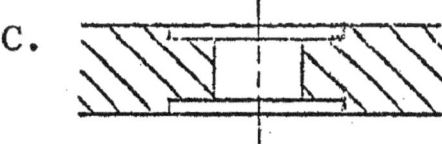
D.

27. When working in a covered trench, the one of the following pieces of equipment that is not permissible to use in the area is a(n)

    A. air-operated jackhammer
    B. air-operated saw
    C. electric-driven saw
    D. gasoline-powered vibrator

27____

28. On a construction job, safety shoes are shoes

    A. with extra hard heels and soles to prevent nails piercing the shoe
    B. with a metal guard over the toes built into the shoe
    C. made of special leather to prevent piercing of the shoe by falling objects
    D. with a plastic liner to protect the feet

28____

29.

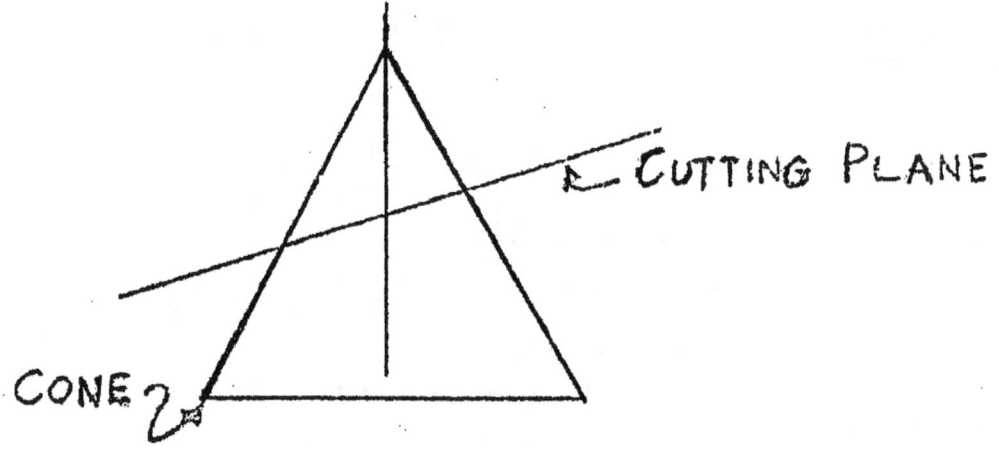

    The shape of the surface created by a plane cutting the right cone as shown above would be a(n)

    A. parabola   B. hyperbola   C. ellipse   D. circle

29____

30. Any section taken through a sphere will appear on the cutting plane as a(n)

    A. circle   B. ellipse   C. oval   D. spheroid

30____

KEY (CORRECT ANSWERS)

1.	C	16.	C
2.	C	17.	C
3.	A	18.	D
4.	D	19.	B
5.	B	20.	B
6.	B	21.	C
7.	D	22.	B
8.	B	23.	C
9.	B	24.	D
10.	A	25.	A
11.	D	26.	A
12.	B	27.	D
13.	B	28.	B
14.	A	29.	C
15.	D	30.	A

EXAMINATION SECTION
TEST 1

DIRECTIONS: Each question or incomplete statement is followed by several suggested answers or completions. Select the one that BEST answers the question or completes the statement. *PRINT THE LETTER OF THE CORRECT ANSWER IN THE SPACE AT THE RIGHT.*

1. In leveling, a backsight on BM *A* is 4.270 and the foresight on TP #1 is 7.384. The elevation of BM *A* is 27.842.
   The HI is

   A. 17.399   B. 32.112   C. 39.213   D. 43.764

2. A bill of materials calls for twenty-four 4" x 10" x 16'0" wooden beams.
   The number of FBM in these beams is

   A. 1210   B. 1230   C. 1250   D. 1280

3. Two kinds of concrete are being used in the construction of a reinforced concrete building. Slump tests show one concrete to have a slump of 7 inches, the other 3 inches. The concrete with the 7 inch slump would be used for

   A. beams   B. floors   C. roof   D. columns

4. A planimeter is used to

   A. measure the area of plane figures
   B. draw parallel lines
   C. measure the distance between parallel lines
   D. measure distances on plans

5. The bearing of line AB is N65°W, that of line AC is S15°E.
   The angle BAC is

   A. 130°   B. 120°   C. 75°   D. 45°

6. In a right triangle, the hypotenuse, AB, is 13 feet long. The side AC is 12 feet and side BC is 5 feet long. A perpendicular is dropped from C to side AB.
   Its length, in feet, in MOST NEARLY

   A. 4.4   B. 4.6   C. 4.9   D. 5.1

7. The roots of the equation $2x^2 - x - 15 = 0$ are

   A. -3.0, +2.5   B. +3.0, -5.0
   C. +1.5, -5.0   D. +3.0, -2.5

8. In laying out a horizontal circular curve for a highway,

   A. the center of the curve must be located on the ground
   B. full stations are located by deflection angles and chord distances
   C. field taping must be done along the arc of the curve
   D. an Engineer's Level must be used

2 (#1)

9. In reinforced concrete construction, the reinforcing bars should be

    A. oiled to prevent rusting
    B. bent while at a red heat
    C. securely fastened so that they will not be displaced during the pour
    D. placed immediately after the concrete is poured

10. The distance between the zero and 100-foot marks of a steel tape is 99.9 feet. To lay out a true distance of 321.7 feet with this tape, the tape distance should be

    A. 319.7   B. 320.5   C. 322.0   D. 323.3

11.

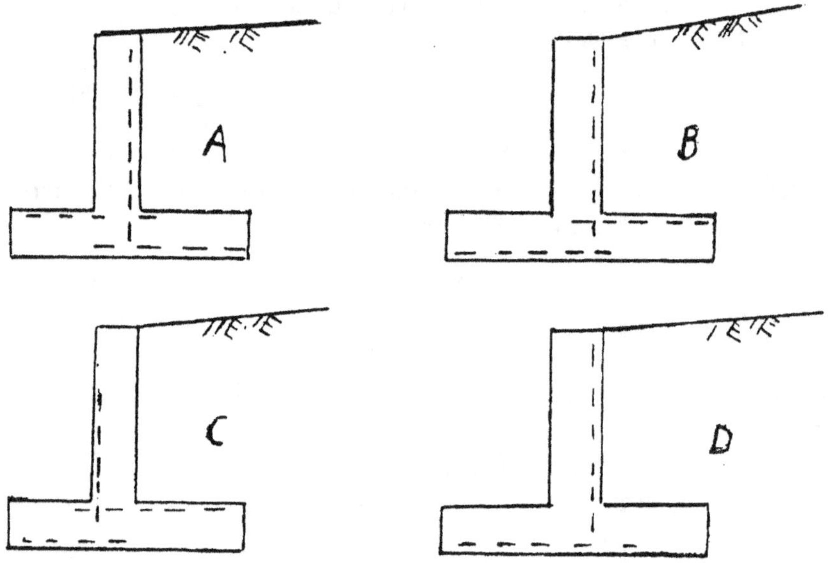

In which one of the cantilever retaining walls shown above is the main reinforcing steel, indicated by the dotted lines, CORRECTLY located?

    A. A   B. B   C. C   D. D

12. The sensitivity of a bubble tube such as those on a transit or that on a level is a function of the

    A. length of the bubble tube
    B. spacing of the graduations on the tube
    C. radius of curvature of the inner surface of the glass forming the top of the tube
    D. length of the bubble within the bubble tube

13. The water pressure at a point 175 feet below the surface is, in pounds per square inch, MOST NEARLY

    A. 76   B. 79   C. 82   D. 85

14. The sum of the interior angles of a five-sided polygon is

    A. 390°   B. 480°   C. 540°   D. 660°

15. A true meridian on a map indicates 15.____

    A. true north
    B. the equator
    C. the latitude
    D. the direction of the magnetic pole

16. Points A, B, and C lie on the circumference of a circle with a 10-inch radius. Angle BAC is 45°. 16.____
    The length of chord BC is, in inches, MOST NEARLY

    A. 8.1   B. 9.1   C. 14.1   D. 15.1

17. The equations of two straight lines are y = 2x + 4 and y = 6 - x. 17.____
    They coordinate of the point of intersection is MOST NEARLY

    A. 5.31   B. 5.33   C. 5.35   D. 5.39

18. Which of the following statements with respect to contour lines is NOT correct? 18.____

    A. Contours crossing streams form vees which point upstream.
    B. A closed contour represents a hill or depression.
    C. Contours never cross except in the case of an overhanging cliff.
    D. The horizontal distance between contours does not vary with the slope of the ground.

19. A bill of material calls for 2 x 4's, S4S. The dressed size of this lumber is, in inches, 19.____

    A. 3 x 5   B. 1 5/8 x 3 7/8   C. 1 3/8 x 3 5/8   D. 1 5/8 x 3 5/8

20. Of the following terms, the one which is LEAST related to the others is 20.____

    A. azimuth   B. camber   C. batter   D. grade

21. The larger the Modulus of elasticity of a material, the 21.____

    A. *greater* the stress it can withstand
    B. *greater* the strain it can withstand
    C. *less* it will be strained for a given stress
    D. *less* it will be stressed for a given strain

22. In a simple reinforced concrete beam in a building, the concrete below the reinforcing steel serves PRIMARILY 22.____

    A. as fire protection
    B. to increase the shearing strength of the beam
    C. to simplify construction
    D. to prevent rusting of the steel

23. The foot-pound is a unit of 23.____

    A. power   B. work   C. force   D. capacity

24. The resistance of a 60 watt 110 volt light bulb is MOST NEARLY, in ohms, 24.____

    A. 60   B. 110   C. 160   D. 200

4 (#1)

25. A horizontal force of 45 pounds is applied to a 60-pound weight which is suspended by a wire. 25._____
When the system is in equilibrium, the tension in the wire is, in pounds,
   A. 75   B. 80   C. 85   D. 90

KEY (CORRECT ANSWERS)

1. B   11. B
2. D   12. C
3. D   13. A
4. A   14. C
5. A   15. A

6. B   16. C
7. D   17. B
8. B   18. D
9. C   19. D
10. C   20. A

21. C
22. A
23. B
24. D
25. A

SOLUTIONS TO PROBLEMS

1. **ANSWER: B**
   The HI is independent of the foresight measurement.
   HI = 27.842 + 4.270 = 32.112

2. **ANSWER: D**
   One board ft. = 144 in.

   NO. of FBM = $\dfrac{(16 \times 12)(4)(10)(24)}{144}$ = 1280

5. **ANSWER: A**
   $\angle BAC = (90 - 65) + 90 + 15$
   $= 130$

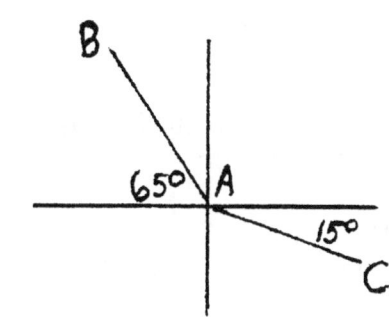

6. **ANSWER: B**
   sin B = 12/13 = y/5
   y = 60/13 = 4.6

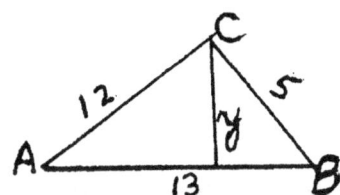

7. **ANSWER: D**
   $(2x+5)(x-3) = 0$
   x = -2.5; x = +3.0

10. **ANSWER: C**
    Error = 100 - 99.9 = 0.1 ft./100 ft. of true length
    ∴ 321.7 + 3(0.1) = 322.0 ft.

13. **ANSWER: A**
    One atmosphere (14.7 psi) = 34 ft. of water
    175/34 = 5.15 atm.
    (5.15)(14.7) = 76 psi.
    (This neglects the 1 atm. above the water surface.)

14. **ANSWER: C**
    For an n-sided polygon, the sum of the interior angles, say 2 a (for a regular polygon), is 2 an.
    2a = 180 - 360/n
    2na = 180n - 360 = 900 - 360 = 540° (for n=5)

16. ANSWER: C
    $AB^2 = BC^2 + CA^2$
    $BC = CA$
    $2CB^2 = AB^2 = (20)^2 - 400"$
    $CB^2 = 400/2 = 200"$
    $CB = \sqrt{200} = 10\sqrt{2}$
    CB 14.14"

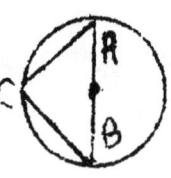

17. ANSWER: B
    $2x+4=6-x$; $x = 2/3$ at intersection
    $y = 2(2/3) + 4 = 5.33$

19. ANSWER: D
    According to American Lumber Standards, trimming of 2 x 4's to S4S means a 3/8 in. loss for each dimension.

21. ANSWER: C
    Modulus of elasticity = stress/strain. For a given stress, the strain decreases as the modulus increases.

23. ANSWER: B
    In general, work is force x distance.

24. ANSWER: D
    $P = VI = I^2R$
    $I = 60/110$; $R = V/I = (110)^2/60 \sim 200$

25. ANSWER: A
    The wire supports all the weight:
    T=75

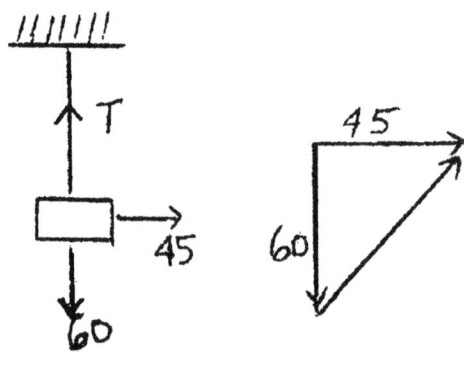

TEST 2

DIRECTIONS: Each question or incomplete statement is followed by several suggested answers or completions. Select the one that BEST answers the question or completes the statement. *PRINT THE LETTER OF THE CORRECT ANSWER IN THE SPACE AT THE RIGHT.*

1. A motor can raise a 3000-pound drop hammer with a velocity of 6 feet per second. Ignoring friction, the horsepower of the motor is

    A. 31.9　　　B. 32.7　　　C. 33.1　　　D. 34.3

    1.____

2. In the system of pulleys shown at the right, the force F required to lift the 500 pound weight, ignoring friction, is MOST NEARLY.
    A. 990
    B. 450
    C. 250
    D. 100

    2.____

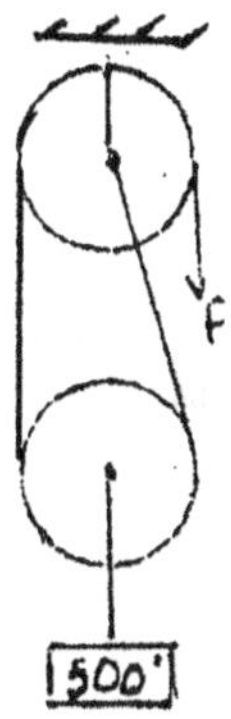

3. A flask weighing 225 grams when empty weighs 446 grams when filled with water and 419 grams when filled with oil. The specific gravity of the oil is about

    A. 0.88　　　B. 0.91　　　C. 0.93　　　D. 0.95

    3.____

4. Piles are NOT driven by

    A. steam hammer　　　B. drop hammer
    C. jack　　　　　　　　D. water hammer

    4.____

5. A protractor is used to

    A. measure area
    B. draw parallel lines
    C. draw guidelines for lettering
    D. measure or layout angles on a scale drawing

    5.____

6. Partial payments totaling $987,500 have been made on a contract of $1,750,000. The percentage of the TOTAL cost paid is

    A. 56.5　　　B. 57.2　　　C. 57.8　　　D. 58.2

    6.____

7. Fire stopping PRIMARILY involves

    A. the placing of incombustible material over surfaces of combustible material
    B. replacing combustible with incombustible material
    C. the use of sprinklers and other protective devices
    D. the subdivision of large dead-air spaces

    7.____

8. The MOST highly stressed rivet in in the gusset plate shown at the right is
   A. A
   B. B
   C. C
   D. D

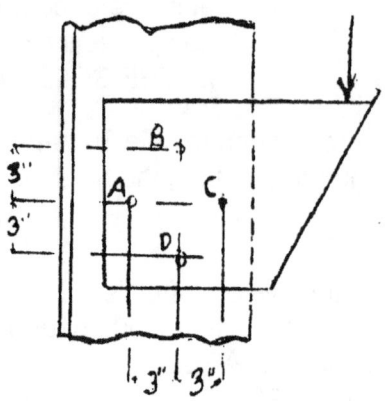

9. The built-in beam shown at the right will bend under load as shown in
   A. A
   B. B
   C. C
   D. D

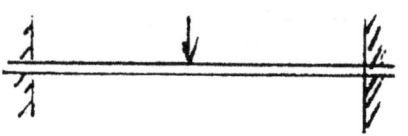

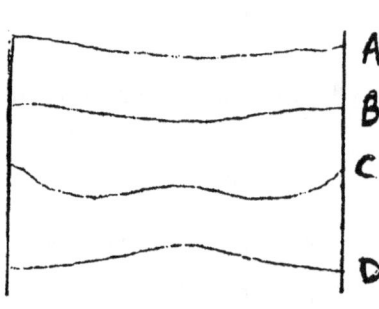

10. A vernier is a device used to
    A. measure fractional parts of a scale division
    B. measure the flow of water
    C. measure fluid pressure
    D. magnify objects

11. Of the following, the BEST pencil to use in taking field notes for a survey is
    A. H   B. 3H   C. 6H   D. 9H

12. A square is inscribed in a circle with a ten-inch diameter. The area of the square, in square inches, is
    A. 52   B. 51   C. 50   D. 49

13. A rectangular box is 10" long, 6" wide, and 4" high. The length of a diagonal drawn from the upper left rear corner to the lower right front corner is, in inches, MOST NEARLY
    A. 12.3   B. 12.4   C. 12.6   D. 12.8

14. A cam is USUALLY a _____ piece.
    A. circular, rotating   B. circular, non-rotating
    C. non-circular, rotating   D. non-circular, non-rotating

15. A right circular cone is 12 inches high, and the diameter of the base is 10 inches. The surface area of the cone is, in square inches, MOST NEARLY

    A. 196   B. 204   C. 210   D. 214

16. Of the following terms, the one which is LEAST related to the others is

    A. spindle   B. key   C. bolt   D. rivet

Questions 17-20.

DIRECTIONS: Each of Questions 17 through 20 is related to one of the lettered items below. Mark the letter of the related item in the space at the right.

17. Sub punch

    A. mortar joint   B. bridging
    C. roofing   D. ream

18. Flashing

    A. mortar joint   B. bridging
    C. roofing   D. ream

19. Joist

    A. mortar joint   B. bridging
    C. roofing   D. ream

20. Point

    A. mortar joint   B. bridging
    C. roofing   D. ream

21. Of the following terms, the one which is LEAST related to the others is

    A. bevel   B. pitch
    C. gage   D. edge distance

22. In differential leveling, the following shots were taken from a single set-up: on T.P.#1, 5.643; on T.P.#2, 8.159. T.P.#1 is _____ than T.P.#2 by _____.

    A. *higher;* 13.802   B. *lower;* 13.802
    C. *higher;* 2.516   D. *lower;* 2.516

23. Of the following terms, the one which is LEAST related to the others is

    A. course   B. stud   C. bat   D. bond

24. A.

B.

C. ─┤₁│₁│₁├─

D. ⏚

In the symbols shown above, the one which represents a battery is

A. A   B. B   C. C   D. D

25. A 6" diameter steel pipe, 100 feet long, installed at 60° F conveys steam at 220° F. If the coefficient of linear expansion is 0.0000065 per degree Fahrenheit, the number of feet that the pipe expands is MOST NEARLY

A. .098   B. .104   C. .108   D. .116

KEY (CORRECT ANSWERS)

1.	B	11.	B
2.	C	12.	C
3.	A	13.	A
4.	D	14.	C
5.	D	15.	B
6.	A	16.	A
7.	D	17.	D
8.	C	18.	C
9.	B	19.	B
10.	A	20.	A

21. A
22. C
23. B
24. C
25. B

SOLUTIONS TO PROBLEMS

1. ANSWER: B
   Power = (3000)(6) = 18,000 ft-lb/sec.
   One HP = 550 ft-lb/sec.
   P = 18,000/550 = 32.7 HP

2. ANSWER: C
   Mechanical advantage = 2
   2F = 500; F = 250

3. ANSWER: A
   Wt. of water = 446 - 225 = 221
   Wt. of oil = 419 - 225 = 194
   Sp. gr. = 194/221 = 0.875

6. ANSWER: A

   $\dfrac{9.875 \times 10^5}{1.75 \times 10^5} \times 10^2 = 56.5\%$

12. ANSWER: C
    Diagonal of square = x/2

    Then $10 = x\sqrt{2}$

    $x = 10\sqrt{2}$

    Field of square = x^2

    $x^2 = (10/\sqrt{2})^2 = 100/2 = 50$
          OR
    A(field of square) = x^2 and
    $x^2 = 5^2 + 5^2 - 50$

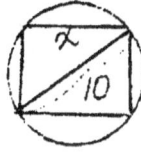

13. ANSWER: A
    $y^2 = 10^2 + 6^2 = 136"$
    $x^2 = y^2 + 4^2 = 152"$
    $x = \sqrt{152} = 12.33"$ (most nearly)

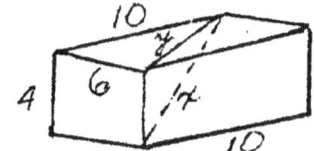

15. ANSWER: B

    The curved surface of a right circular cone is $\pi r\sqrt{r^2 + h^2}$

    A = $(\pi)(5)\sqrt{25+144} = 65\pi \sim 204$ (does not include area of the base)

22. ANSWER: C
    The larger number read on the scale refers to the lower level: 8.159 - 5.643 = 2.516

25. ANSWER: B
    Expansion = (100 ft.)(220 - 60°)(6.5 x 10^{-6}) - 0.104 ft.

TEST 3

DIRECTIONS: Each question or incomplete statement is followed by several suggested answers or completions. Select the one that BEST answers the question or completes the statement. *PRINT THE LETTER OF THE CORRECT ANSWER IN THE SPACE AT THE RIGHT.*

1. [Four square symbols labeled A, B, C, D showing different section hatching patterns]

    Of the symbols shown above for materials in section, the one representing glass is

    A. A   B. B   C. C   D. D

    1.____

2. Of the symbols shown in the question above, for materials in section, the one representing cast iron is

    A. A   B. B   C. C   D. D

    2.____

Questions 3-6.

DIRECTIONS: Each of Questions 3 through 6 is related but in an opposite sense to one of the items marked A, B, C, and D. As an example, the terms *longitudinal* and *transverse* are related in that they both refer to direction, but, of course, the directions are at right angles. Indicate in the space at the right the OPPOSITE to the terms in these questions.

3. Tap

    A. Mantissa   B. Departure   C. Spiget   D. Die

    3.____

4. Bell

    A. Mantissa   B. Departure   C. Spiget   D. Die

    4.____

5. Latitude

    A. Mantissa   B. Departure   C. Spiget   D. Die

    5.____

6. Characteristic

    A. Mantissa   B. Departure   C. Spiget   D. Die

    6.____

Questions 7-11.

DIRECTIONS: In each of the following groups of drawings, the top view and front elevation of an object are shown at the left. At the right are four drawings, one of which represents the end elevation of the object as seen from the right. Select the drawing which represents the CORRECT end elevation.

NOTE: The first group is shown as a sample only. Which drawing represents the CORRECT end elevation?

A. A   B. B   C. C   D. D

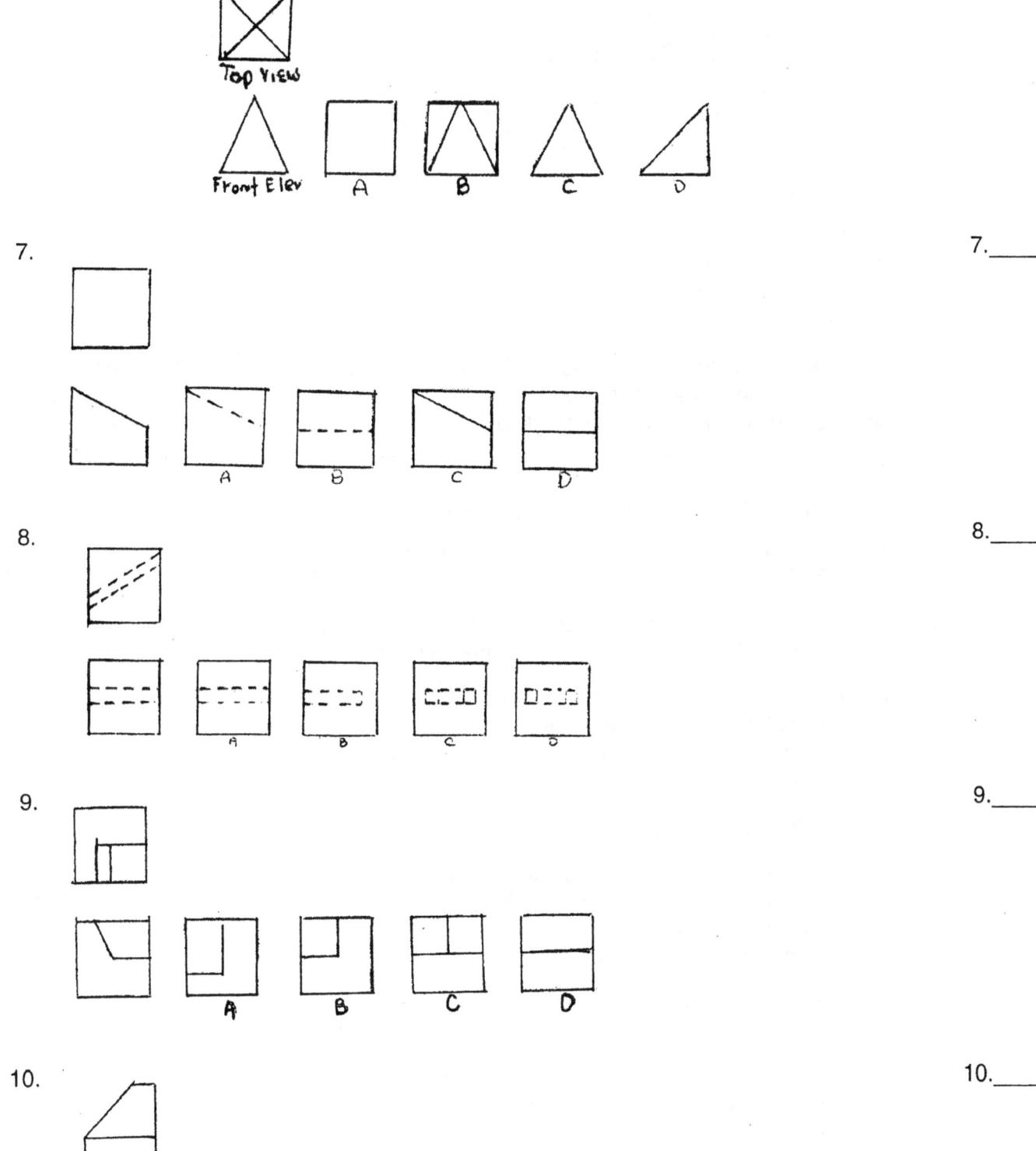

11.

[Figure: top view of a pyramid-like shape; below are four options A, B, C, D showing different side/perspective views]

12. Ten-penny nails

    A. are 10 inches long
    B. cost 10 cents per dozen
    C. weigh 10 pounds per thousand
    D. are not a commercial size

13. A dimension on a blueprint marked 3'4" is scaled and found to be 1 1/4". A second dimension on the same print scales 2 7/16".
The second dimension should be marked

    A. 6'3"   B. 6'6"   C. 6'8"   D. 6'9"

14. The logarithm of 2 is 0.30103. The logarithm of 0.25 is

    A. 9.39689-10   B. 9.39791-10
    C. 9.39793-10   D. 9.39796-10

15. A 1:2:3 1/2 concrete has a water-cement ratio of 6 gallons per sack of cement. The strength of the concrete can be increased by decreasing the

    A. ratio of the fine aggregate to cement
    B. ratio of the coarse aggregate to cement
    C. ratio of both fine and coarse aggregate to cement
    D. water-cement ratio

16. A spiral easement curve is NOT used

    A. to connect a tangent and a circular curve
    B. to connect two circular curves of different radii
    C. to connect two tangents
    D. at any time in highway work

17. Batter boards are used to

    A. define construction lines on the ground
    B. prevent splatter of concrete when pouring
    C. absorb shock in construction work
    D. barricade the construction area

18. In surveying, *double hubbing* or *double reversing* is done with a

    A. transit   B. level   C. tape   D. alidado

19. The inner surfaces of forms for concrete are oiled

    A. to prevent rusting
    B. to make removal of forms easier
    C. to prevent honeycombing
    D. when a stiff concrete mixture is being used

20. Installation of a sprinkler system would be LEAST complicated when the type of building construction is

    A. flat slab   B. beam and girder
    C. steel frame   D. brick bearing wall

21. Of the following items, the one which is NOT an opening protective is fire

    A. door   B. tower   C. shutter   D. window

22. A load is to be supported by two 2 x 4's on a long simple span. The BEST way to arrange the 2 x 4's for maximum strength is

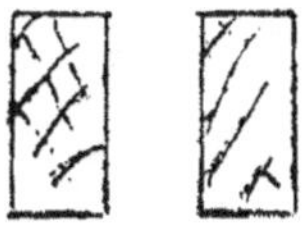

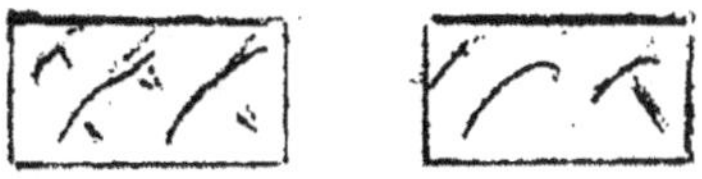

Questions 23-24.

DIRECTIONS: Questions 23 and 24 are to be answered on the basis of the truss shown below.

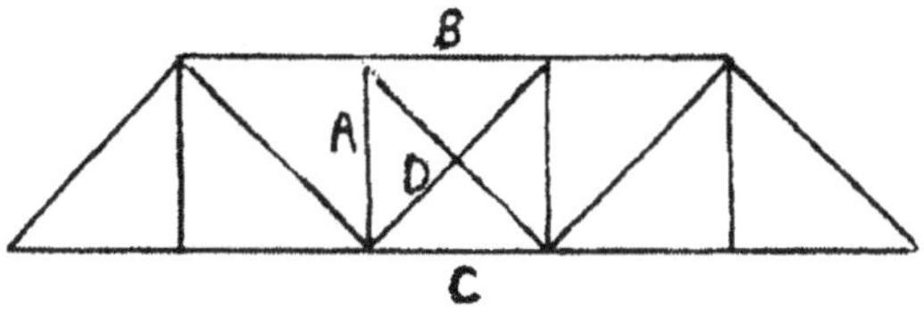

23. The compression chord member is marked

    A. A   B. B   C. C   D. D

24. The tension chord member is marked

    A. A   B. B   C. C   D. D

25. A small by-pass on a large gate valve serves PRIMARILY

    A. to reduce the unbalanced pressure on the gate when opening the valve
    B. as a by-pass in case the valve cannot be opened
    C. to meter the flow through the valve
    D. to tell which way the water is flowing

KEY (CORRECT ANSWERS)

1. B
2. D
3. D
4. C
5. B

6. A
7. D
8. C
9. B
10. A

11. A
12. C
13. B
14. C
15. D

16. C
17. A
18. A
19. B
20. A

21. B
22. A
23. B
24. C
25. A

SOLUTIONS TO PROBLEMS

7. ANSWER: D
   The perspective drawings are as follows:

   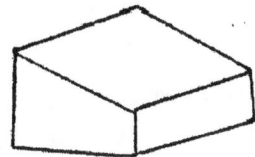

8. ANSWER: C

   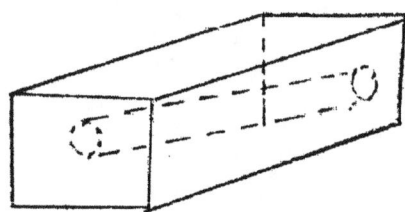

9. ANSWER: B

   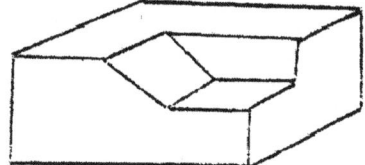

10. ANSWER: A

    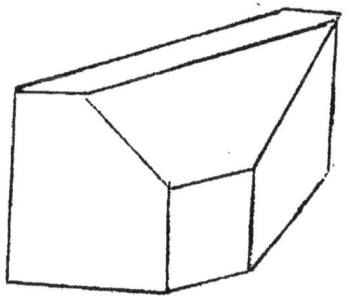

    (As seen from rear of front elevation)

11. ANSWER: A

    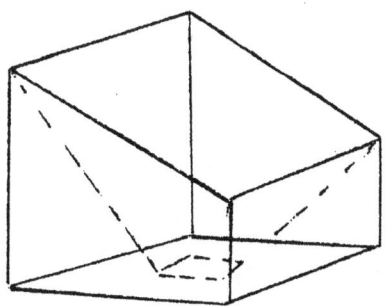

13. ANSWER: B
    Scale = 5/4 in. per 40 in. = 1/32 in./in.
    At a scale of 2 7/16 in., the second dimension is
    (39/16)(32) = 78 in. = 6'6"

14. ANSWER: C
    Log (1/4) = log 2^{-2} = (-2 x 0.30103) = 0.60206
                                                         = 9.39794-10

TEST 4

DIRECTIONS: Each question or incomplete statement is followed by several suggested answers or completions. Select the one that BEST answers the question or completes the statement. *PRINT THE LETTER OF THE CORRECT ANSWER IN THE SPACE AT THE RIGHT.*

1. The joints of bell-and-spigot cast iron water mains are filled with

    A. lead   B. copper   C. rubber   D. oakum

2. Parallax exists in a transit when the

    A. line of sight is parallel to the long bubble
    B. cross-hairs appear to move over the object sighted when the observer's eye is moved slightly
    C. line of sight is perpendicular to the horizontal axis
    D. vertical axis is perpendicular to the horizontal axis

3. In unlined tunnel work, survey points are USUALLY located on

    A. the roof
    B. the walls
    C. the floor
    D. suspended platforms

4. The grit chamber of a sewage plant removes heavy solids such as sand by

    A. allowing the sewage to flow over a weir
    B. reducing the velocity of flow
    C. stopping the flow completely
    D. screens

5. Small sewer pipe is USUALLY made of

    A. cast iron, cement lined
    B. steel
    C. concrete
    D. vitrified clay

6. A timber weighing 500 pounds is to be dragged over a stone floor with a rope which makes an angle of 45 with the horizontal.
   If the coefficient of static friction is 0.4, the tension in the rope necessary to start the timber moving is, in pounds, MOST NEARLY

    A. 196   B. 202   C. 208   D. 214

7. A stadia survey would MOST probably be made in connection with

    A. a building layout
    B. a topographic map
    C. the location of bridge piers
    D. the erection of steel

8. The flanges and web of an H-section 12" wide by 12" deep are one inch thick. Steel weighs 490 pounds per cubic foot.
   A 10'0" length of this column would weigh, in pounds, MOST NEARLY

    A. 1150   B. 1250   C. 1350   D. 1450

9. The term *bond,* as used in connection with brick work, refers to the

   A. adhesion of mortar to brick
   B. metal anchors used to tie beams to wall
   C. arrangement of the bricks within the wall
   D. ties used to hold the brick to the backing

10. [sketch: loads of 10,000; 20,000; 20,000 at distances 8'0" and 12'0"]

    The center of gravity of the three concentrated loads shown in the sketch above is located a distance, in feet, from the right load of

    A. 8.4 B. 8.6 C. 8.8 D. 9.0

11. A Philadelphia Rod which can be used with or without a target

    A. is a sighting pole used for line work
    B. has a movable ribbon
    C. has a pointed shoe
    D. has graduations 0.01 feet wide

12. An airplane is flying at 240 mph (air speed). A wind of 100 mph is blowing at right angles to the longitudinal axis of the plane.
    The ground speed of the airplane is, in mph,

    A. 220 B. 240 C. 260 D. 280

Questions 13-17.

DIRECTIONS: Each of Questions 13 through 17 is related to one of the lettered items below. Indicate the CORRECT answer.

13. Fillet

    A. buck   B. cable   C. parapet
    D. bond   E. weld   F. plaster

14. Coping

    A. buck   B. cable   C. parapet
    D. bond   E. weld   F. plaster

15. Jamb

    A. buck   B. cable   C. parapet
    D. bond   E. weld   F. plaster

16. Stretcher

    A. buck   B. cable   C. parapet
    D. bond   E. weld   F. plaster

17. Bx

    A. buck   B. cable   C. parapet
    D. bond   E. weld   F. plaster

18. A block of wood of specific gravity 0.6 weighs 10 pounds. Its volume, in cubic feet, is MOST NEARLY

    A. .027   B. 0.27   C. 2.7   D. 27

19. A rectangular barge weighs 1,000,000 pounds when fully loaded and has outside dimensions of 60 feet long, 30 feet wide, and 10 feet deep.
    In fresh water, it sinks to a depth, in feet, MOST NEARLY of

    A. 7.7   B. 7.9   C. 8.9   D. 9.9

20. A gas in a compressor cylinder under an absolute pressure of 14.7 pounds per square inch has a volume of 6 cubic inches. It is compressed so slowly that its temperature does not vary, to a pressure of 100 pounds per square inch absolute.
    Its volume now is, in cubic inches, MOST NEARLY

    A. 0.58   B. 0.68   C. 0.78   D. 0.88

21. A quantity of mercury is heated, and Fahrenheit and Centigrade thermometers are immersed in it. The reading on the Fahrenheit scale is exactly twice the reading on the centigrade scale.
    The reading on the Fahrenheit scale is

    A. 320   B. 360   C. 400   D. 440

22. A piece of metal 6 inches in diameter is being turned in a lathe.
    If the recommended cutting speed is 500 feet per minute, the required revolutions per minute of the spindle is MOST NEARLY

    A. 320   B. 2130   C. 1320   D. 120

23. A building is being raised by a jack preparatory to underpinning the structure. The load on the jack is 4000 pounds. The jack screw has a pitch of 2 threads per inch.
    Ignoring friction, the force, in pounds, applied at a point on a capstan bar 3'0" from the axis of the jack screw required to raise the building is MOST NEARLY

    A. 288   B. 144   C. 72   D. 9

24. Of the following items, the one that is LEAST related to the others in function is

    A. bulldozer   B. clamshell
    C. backhoe   D. A-frame

25. One pound of lead at 200° F is placed in one pound of water which is at a temperature of 60° F. In a short time, both attain the same temperature of 64.3.
    The specific heat of lead as determined above, in BTU per pound per degree Fahrenheit, is MOST NEARLY

    A. .0137   B. .0217   C. .0317   D. .0537

KEY (CORRECT ANSWERS)

1.	A	11.	D
2.	B	12.	C
3.	A	13.	E
4.	B	14.	C
5.	D	15.	A
6.	B	16.	D
7.	B	17.	B
8.	A	18.	B
9.	C	19.	C
10.	C	20.	D

21. A
22. A
23. D
24. D
25. C

SOLUTIONS TO PROBLEMS

6. **ANSWER: B**
   F = kN, where N = normal force between the surfaces, and
   k = coefficient of static friction
   ∴ F min. = (500)(0.4) = 200

   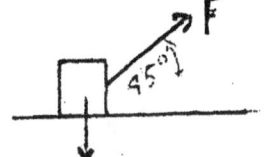

8. **ANSWER: A**
   Two sections have volume,
   $V_1 = (10)(1)(1/12)$.
   One section has $V_2 = (10/12)(1/12)(10)$
   Weight = $(2V_1 + V_2)(490) \sim 1150$

   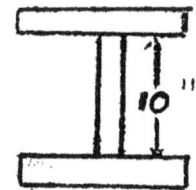

10. **ANSWER: C**
    50,000x = (20,000)(12)+(10,000)(20) x = 8.8

    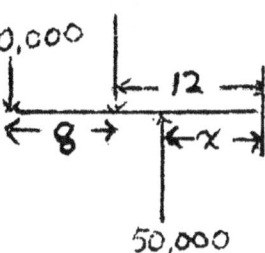

12. **ANSWER: C**
    $V = \sqrt{100^2 + 200^2} = 260$

    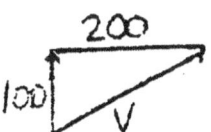

18. **ANSWER: B**
    Density = (0.6)(62.4) lb./ft.^{3}
    Volume = 10/(0.6)(62.4) ~ 0.27

19. **ANSWER: C**
    10^6 lbs. will displace 106/62.4 = 1.6 x 10^4 ft.^{3} of water.
    Since cross section = 60 x 30 ft.^{2}, depth = 1.6 x 10^4/60 x30 = 8.9 ft.

20. **ANSWER: D**
    Boyle's law: PV = constant
    (14.7)(6)   = (100 x V)
           V = 0.882 ft.^{3}

21. **ANSWER: A**
    In general, °F. = (9/5)° C + 32
    When F = 2C,
    ∴   F = (9/5)(F/2) + 32
         F = 320°

22. **ANSWER: A**

    The initial circumference of the piece is $\pi D = \pi/2$ ft.

    ∴ $500/(\pi/2) = 320$ ft. per min.

23. **ANSWER: D**

    The mechanical advantage of a screw or jack =

    $2\pi l/p$ (l = length of force arm, p = pitch of the screw)

    Mech. Adv. = $(2\pi)(36)/0.5 = 144\pi$.

    Force = $4000/144\pi \sim 9$ lb.

24. **ANSWER: C**

    $Q = m C_p \Delta t$

    For water, $C_p = 1$ Btu/lb./°F.
    $(1.0)(1.0)(64.3 - 60) = (1.0)(C_p)(200 - 64.3)$
    $C_p = 4.3/135.7 = 0.0317$

ABSTRACT REASONING
SPATIAL RELATIONS / THREE DIMENSIONS

COMMENTARY

Since intelligence exists in many forms or phases and the theory of differential aptitudes is now firmly established in testing, other manifestations and measurements of intelligence than verbal or purely arithmetical must be identified and measured.

The spatial relations test, including that phase designated as spatial perception, involves and measures the ability to solve problems, drawn up in the form of outlines or pictures, which are concerned with the shapes of objects or the interrelationship of their parts. While, concededly, little is known about the nature and scope of this aptitude, it appears that this ability is required in science, mathematics, engineering, and drawing courses and curricula. Accordingly, tests of spatial perception involving the reconstruction of three-dimensional pair-terns, are presented in this section.

It is to be noted that the relationships expressed in spatial tests are geometric, definitive, and exact. Keeping these basic characteristics in mind, the applicant is to proceed to solve the spatial perception problems in his own way. There is no set method of solving these problems. The examinee may find that there are different methods for different types of spatial problems. Therefore, the BEST way to prepare for this type of test is to take and study the work-practice problems in three-dimensional patterns provided in this section.

SAMPLE QUESTION

In question 1 through 30 a flat pattern will be presented. This pattern is to be folded into a three dimensional figure. The correct figure is one of the four given at the right of the pattern. There is only one correct figure in each set. The outside of the pattern is what is seen at the left.

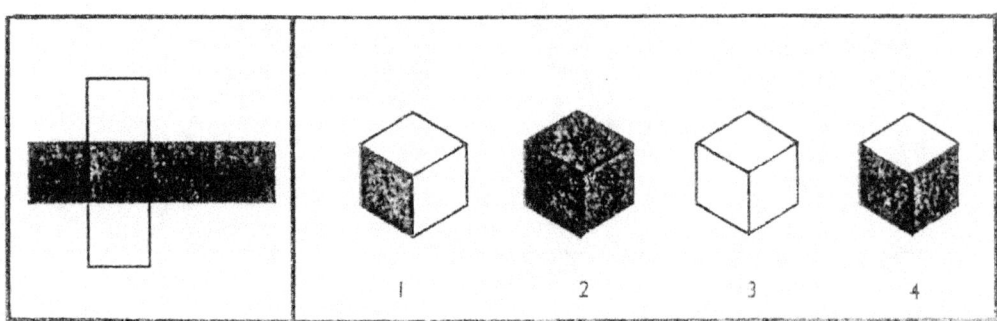

One of the above figures (1,2,3,4) can be formed from the flat pattern given at the left. The only figure that corresponds in the pattern is 4. If the shaded surfaces are looked at as the sides of the box, then all four sides must be shaded, while the top and bottom are white.

EXAMINATION SECTION

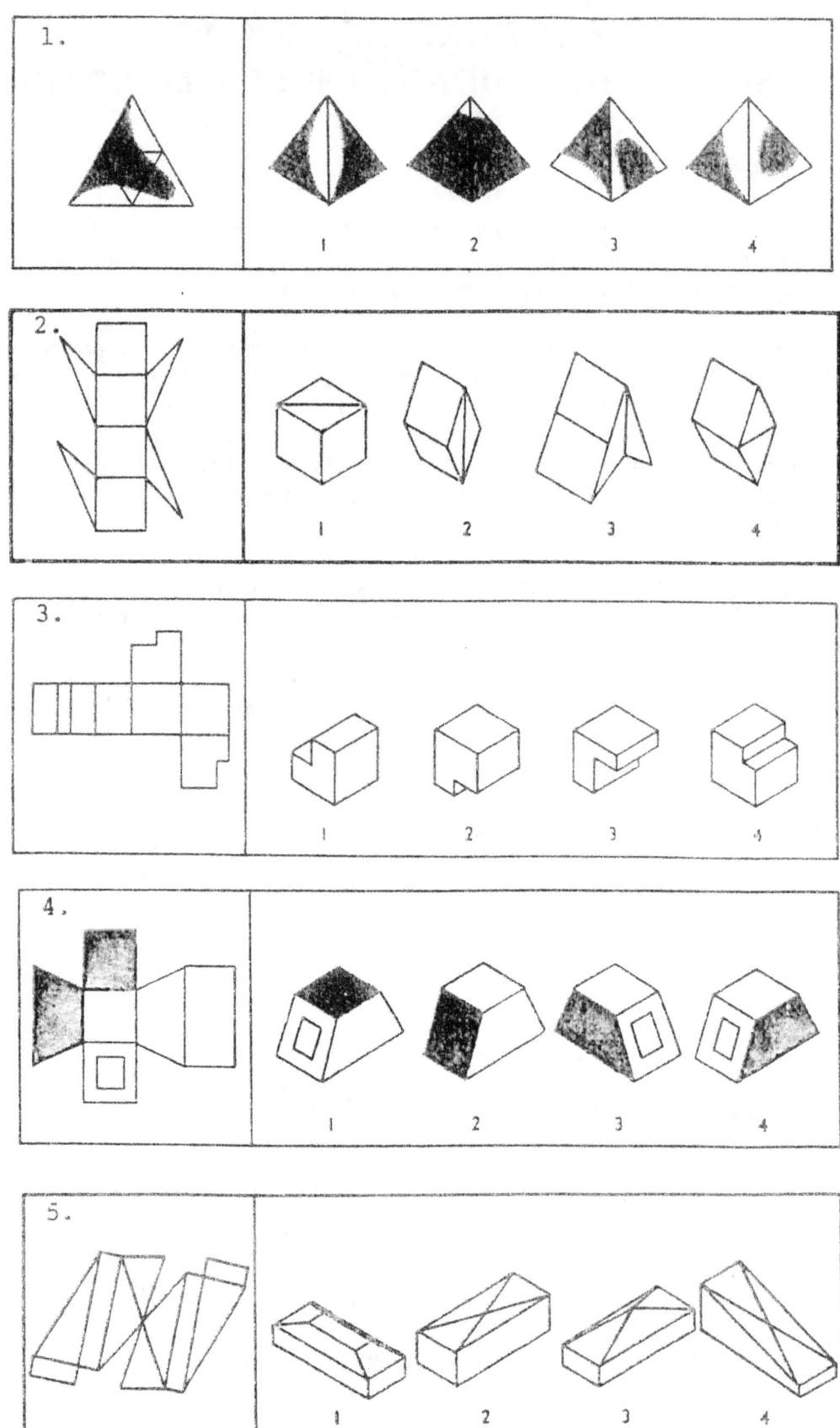

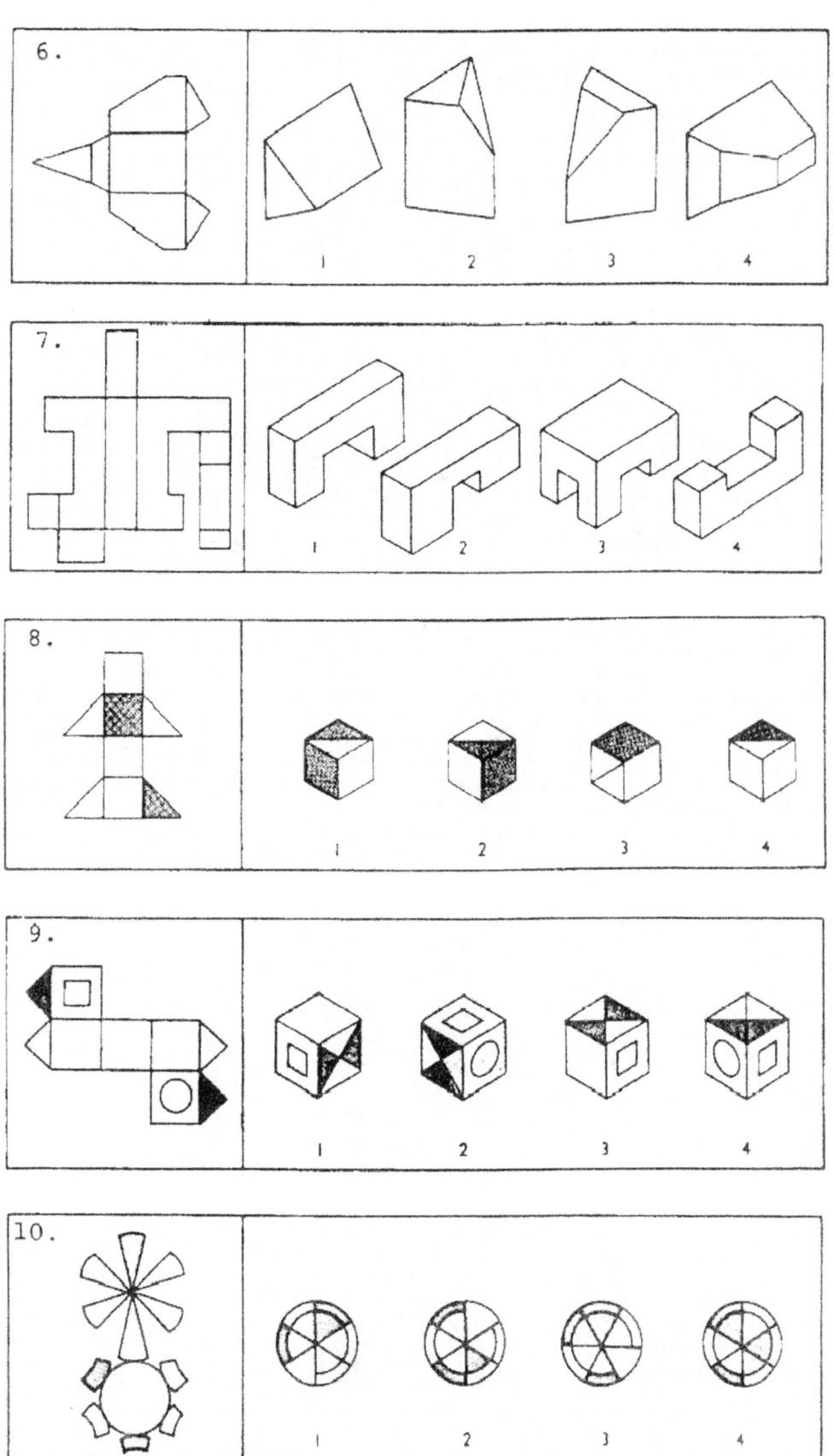

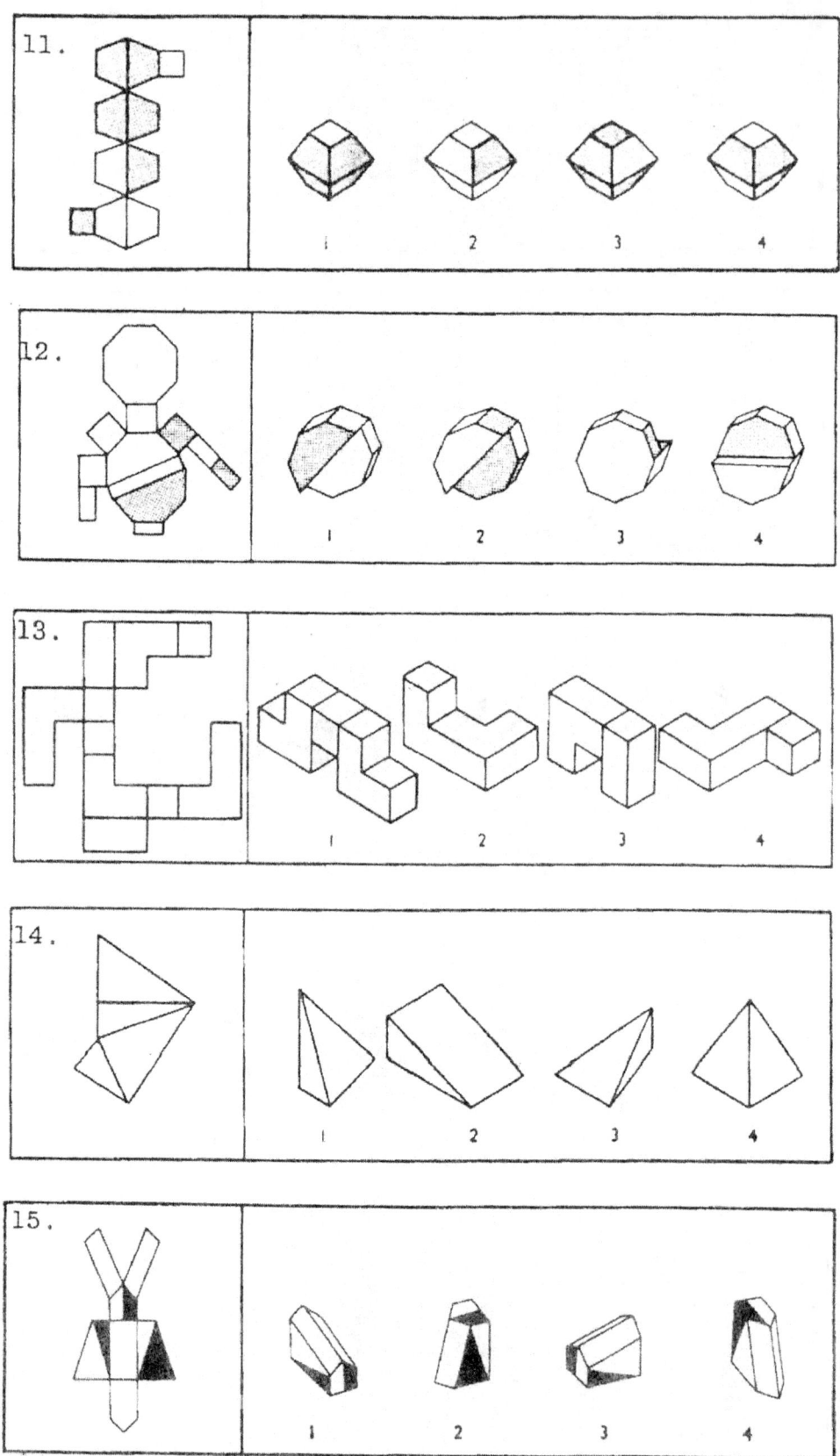

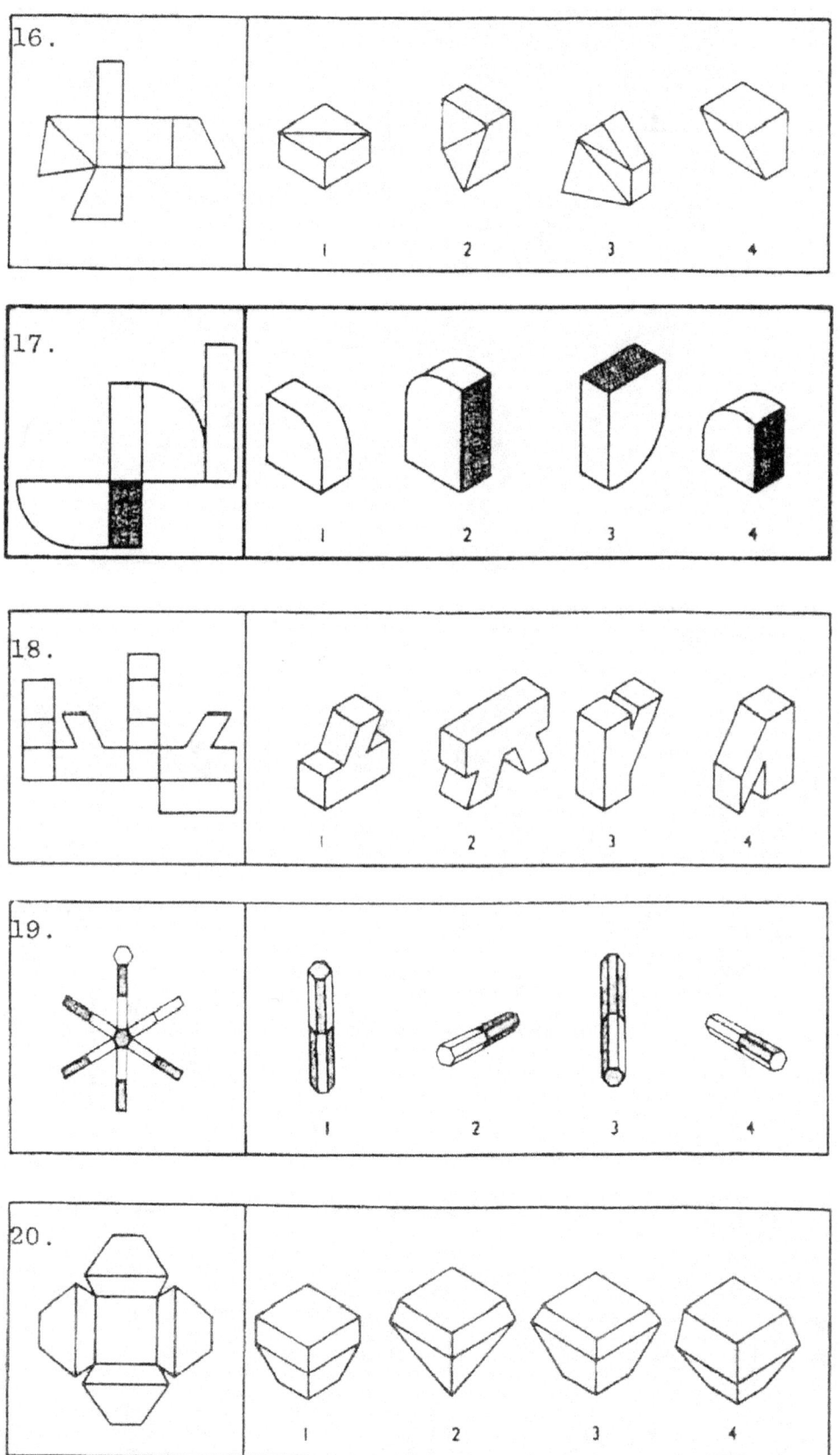

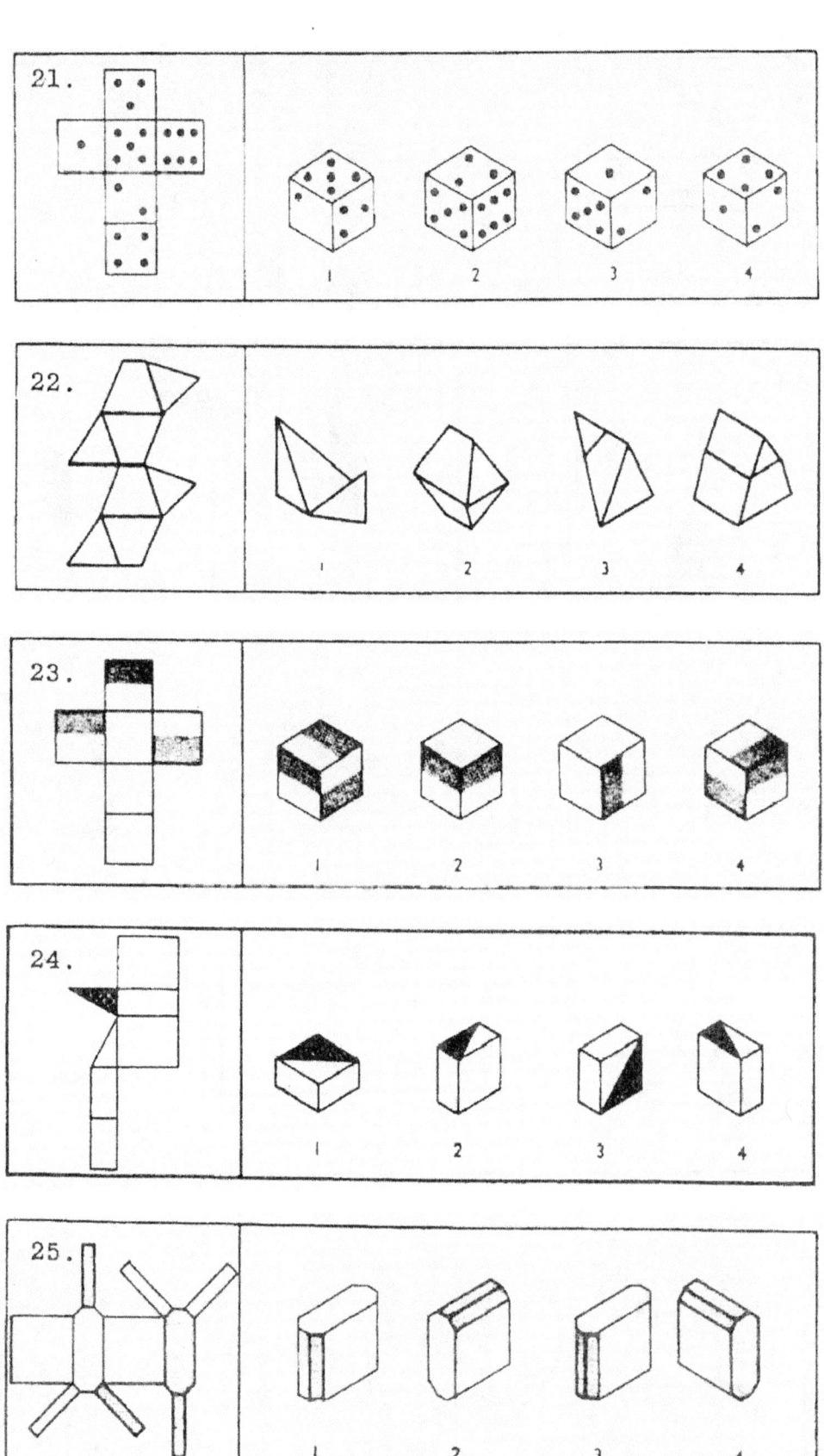

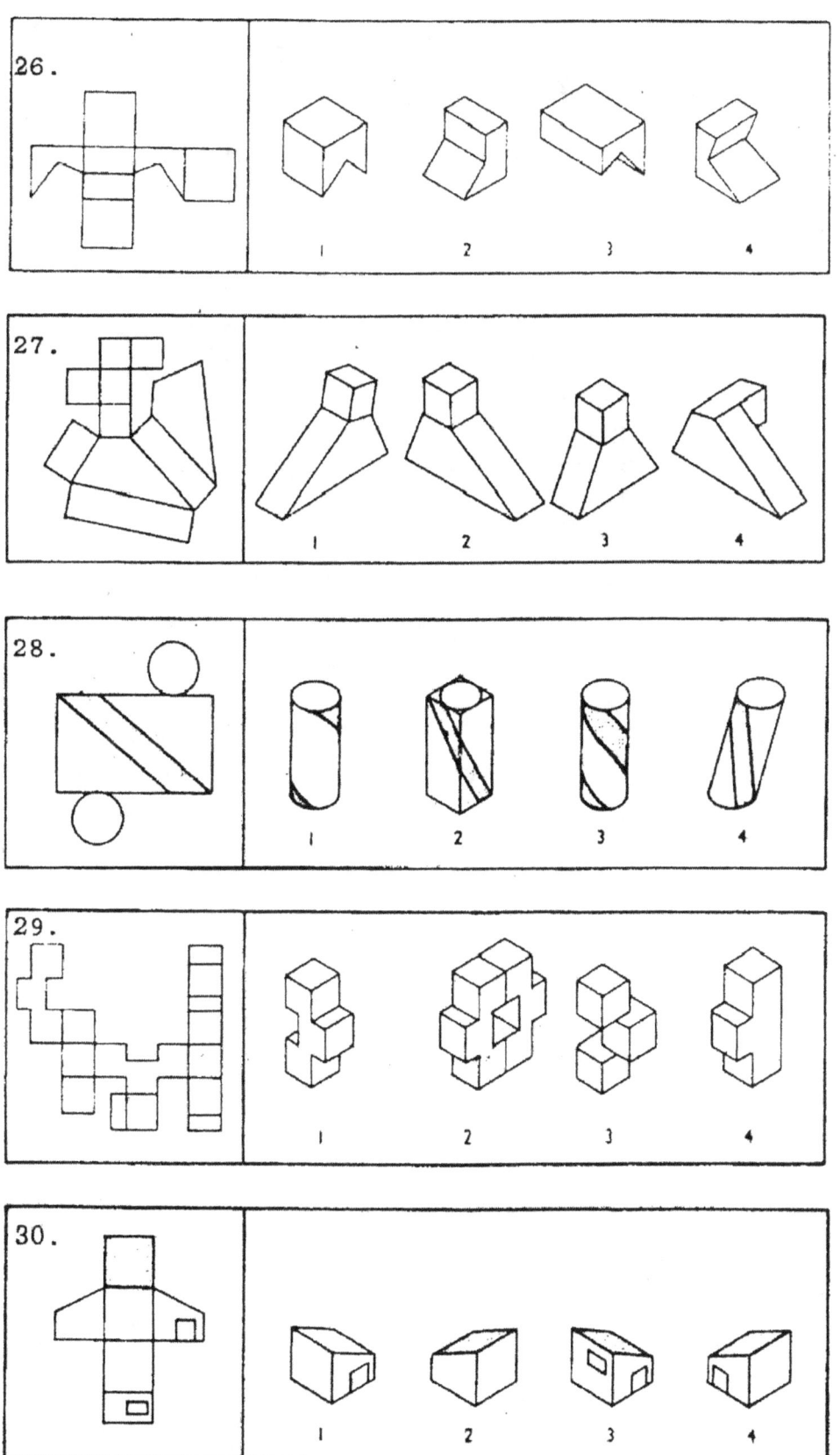

KEY (CORRECT ANSWERS)

1.	4	16.	2
2.	2	17.	3
3.	2	18.	1
4.	3	19.	4
5.	3	20.	3
6.	3	21.	2
7.	4	22.	2
8.	1	23.	3
9.	1	24.	4
10.	1	25.	3
11.	1	26.	4
12.	2	27.	1
13.	2	28.	1
14.	1	29.	1
15.	1	30.	2